THE IMPORTANCE OF REPENTANCE

By

Dr. Steve Davis

Copyright © 2025
All Rights Reserved. Dr. Steve Davis

No Part of this book may be produced, stored in a retrieval system, or transmitted by any means without the written permission of the author.

Copyright Case ID:1-14808259251
All scripture is NIV, unless otherwise noted.

This book is dedicated to my dear friends, George Stidham and Glenn Grindstaff. Over the years, George and I engaged in profound conversations about the concept of repentance. I am deeply grateful for his unwavering prayers and insightful ideas throughout the writing process, and I cherish the fact that he was able to read the completed manuscript before his passing.

Glenn, a deacon at the church where I serve as pastor, played a pivotal role in inspiring this project. One day, he simply asked if I had ever considered writing a book, prompting me to reflect and pray about it. Through this journey, God directed my thoughts toward this important topic.

My heartfelt thanks go to George and Glenn for your invaluable friendship, prayers, and inspiration. Your support has made this work possible.

Table of Contents

INTRODUCTION

CHAPTER 1: JESUS AND REPENTANCE   10
JESUS AND THE LOST SHEEP   15
ZACCHAEUS AND REPENTANCE   17
A WOMAN CAUGHT IN ADULTERY   20
REPENTANCE WITH THE RICH MAN AND LAZARUS   23
REPENTANCE AND JOHN THE BAPTIST   25

CHAPTER 2: THE IMPACTS OF SIN AND GOD'S DISCIPLINE   31
IMPACTS OF SIN   31
CAN REPENTANCE BE PRE-PLANNED   32
THE IMPORTANCE OF GOD'S DISCIPLINE   33
GOD DOES THE CHANGING   39

CHAPTER 3: REPENTANCE IN THE OLD TESTAMENT   41
REPENTANCE IN JACOB'S FAMILY   41
THE BROTHERS NEED FOR MORE REPENTANCE   45
ESAU: SEEKING REPENTANCE BUT NOT FINDING IT   49
REPENTANCE AND EMOTION   53
REPENTANCE WITH DAVID AND SAUL   62
DAVID   70
THE DIFFERENCE BETWEEN SAUL AND DAVID   78
THE OLD TESTAMENT PROPHETS   80

CHAPTER 4: REPENTANCE IN THE BOOKS OF ACTS AND THE EPISTLES — 85

REPENTANCE IN THE BOOK OF ACTS — 86

REPENTANCE IN ROMANS — 89

REPETANCE IN I AND II CORINTHIANS — 93

REPENTANCE IN THE SHORTER EPISTLES — 97

REPENTANCE IN REVELATION — 101

CHAPTER 5: HISTORICAL VIEWS OF REPENTANCE AND THEIR APPLICATION — 103

PRACTICE OF REPENTANCE IN THE BIBLE — 103

REPENTANCE IN THE 3RD AND 4TH CENTURIES — 107

THREE TYPES OF REPENTANCE — 108

THE IMPACT OF TRUE REPENTANCE — 109

FORCED REPENTANCE — 112

FALSE REPENTANCE — 112

FALSE AND LASTING REPENTANCE: A TALE OF TWO KINGS — 116

REPENTANCE IS NECESSARY FOR ALL — 120

SANCTIFICATION — 122

THE IMPORTANCE OF THE BIBLE — 123

REPENTANCE AND CHURCH — 124

TWO QUESTIONS — 126

APPENDIX: BIBLICAL SALVATION — 127

INTRODUCTION

There seems to be something wrong with the world in regards to repentance. I think many people can see this problem although they may not say it that way specifically. It seems today that there are many people who would confess faith in Christ and yet their lifestyle does not match up with what is taught in the Bible. Since we did not live in past times it is difficult to say if this is a modern problem or if it has always been. However, we can definitely see it in our culture today.

If you are like me, you have met a variety of people who claim to be a Christian but somehow it does not ring true. While we cannot judge what has happened in the heart of another person, it seems that the missing element is repentance or being willing to turn away from our sins. We can read these words that Jesus said from Mark 1:14-15: "After John was put in prison, Jesus went into Galilee, proclaiming the good news of God. 'The time has come,' he said. 'The kingdom of God has come near. Repent and believe the good news.'" The message that Jesus preached was clearly a message of belief and repentance and yet, somehow, we have come to the point where we emphasize belief but rarely talk about the subject of repentance.

Before we go on it would be helpful to better understand what repentance is and what repentance is not. Repentance is the idea of having sorrow for our sin and having a desire to change. If a person only has sorrow for their sin then this is not true repentance. Repentance includes the idea of turning from something. When someone is only sorry for their sin and the pain that it has caused themselves and others then they are on their way to repentance. However, biblical repentance is not reached until the individual is both sorry for their sin and has a desire to change and move away from sin.

Webster's dictionary gives this definition for repentance: "to feel sorrow for one's sin and make up one's mind to do what is right." It seems that the idea of making up one's mind to do right is often missed. As well, the definition on Wikipedia is similar which states: "Repentance is reviewing one's actions and feeling contrition or regret for past wrongs, which is accompanied by commitment to and actual actions that show and prove a change for the better." I would agree with both of these in that they convey the idea of having a desire to change and do what is right in the future. It seems that worldly sources have the right idea about repentance. Again, these give the idea that true repentance is not reached until an individual recognizes their sin, is sorry for it AND has a desire to move away from their sinful pattern. It is interesting that these are both secular definitions and yet they seem to understand the idea that repentance involves a willingness to change while many Christians seem to somehow miss this crucial aspect.

We can look at a portrayal in popular culture as an example. Many of us are familiar with how things are portrayed in movies. One of the popular themes is of a mobster who commits a crime in the evening and then goes to confession the next morning only to commit the same crime the next evening. It seems that the mobster goes out to commit the same crime but believes that everything is fine with their soul now because they have confessed their sin. Whether or not this happens very often in real life it is something that is portrayed in popular culture. We seem to instinctively know something is wrong with this picture but may have a hard time putting our finger on it. The problem with this scenario is that the mobster has not had a desire to turn away from sin. Simply confessing sin and seeking forgiveness without having a desire to change will have the outcome of the mobster returning to his sin over and over again. Of course, this is in contrast to the type of repentance that Jesus was talking about. In John 8:11 Jesus tells a woman who was caught in adultery to 'go, and sin no more.' That is the key that is missing in the fictional mobster story. The mobster has no desire to follow Jesus' mandate to 'go, and sin no more' but fully intends to commit the sin again. Therefore, true repentance has not occurred. If we look around we can see this same type of storyline playing out in real lives today. Whether it is the sin of sexual immorality, dishonesty or unforgiveness; each time a person fails to turn away from sin that has been revealed to them then they are essentially doing the same thing that the fictional mobster is doing. When we come to God seeking forgiveness we need to not only confess our sin and trust in Christ for forgiveness but also have a desire to change.

One of the helpful ways that I like to think about repentance is having a desire to be able to go back in time to change my act or attitude so that I did not commit the sin. When we think back about any sin that the Holy Spirit has revealed to us, we need to have the desire to change it. We need to be able to go back through our life and wish that we could change what happened in order for there to be true repentance. Think back about every time you have been dishonest, had an immoral thought, lashed out in anger at someone, refused to forgive someone or been jealous. In order for there to be true repentance we need to say that if we could go back in time to the moment we committed the sin we would change the situation and not commit the sin. Too often we think back about past sins with some type of nostalgia and know deep in our hearts if we could live in that situation again we would desire to do the same thing. When we are thinking like this then we have not truly repented.

When I think about it this type of situation I think of someone I know quite well. They would say that they are a Christian and, again, no one can say for sure what has happened in another person's heart. However, when they talk about past sin I get the impression that they are reveling in those seemingly fun times in their life. This individual had lived an outwardly sinful life in their younger days with a lifestyle of immorality and overindulgence in alcohol. Once these sins have been repented of and we have trusted in Christ then God no longer holds us accountable for them. However, this person talks about those times as if they were good times and they would like to relive them if given the opportunity. As well, when they do something today that is obviously against what God has said in the Bible they tend to brush it off as if it is no big deal. Whenever we do something that is directly in contrast to God's Word then it is a big deal and we need to be sorry for the sin and desire to turn away from it. These things are what make me concerned for this person. They show no signs of being repentant of past sins or even sins that are being committed now. I think we all know people who have this type of attitude. They have a knowledge of God and what Jesus did when He died and rose again as the perfect sacrifice for sins but the missing element is that they have not repented of their sin.

Before we further investigate repentance we need to understand that the word does have a duel meaning. To begin with, we should look at the Greek word in the New Testament that is translated as repent. That word is metanoeo and it is composed of two parts. The first part is meta and it means to change. So, the word for repentance means to change something, but what? The second part of the word is noeo and this means the inner self. Thus, when the New Testament, and Jesus, speak about repentance the meaning is a change in the inner self or how one views the world. This means that one repents of their view about salvation and comes to believe that faith in Christ is the way to salvation that God has ordained. However, many people stop with this meaning while there is another meaning presented in the Bible. By investigating Scripture we will find that repentance means to change how one believes about Christ and also to change their sinful actions and attitudes. As well, these two ideas about repentance, changing belief and actions, are coupled together so that one should not take place without the other. Thus, the change that begins in the inner self will eventually be presented to the world as an outward change in actions.

One important note about repentance that we should discuss before we move deeper into the topic is the role of the Holy Spirit. The Holy

Spirt is the third person of the Trinity and so He is fully God. Part of His role is to convict people of sin and to help them to overcome temptation. When we come to God in repentance we are asked to be willing to change and put our faith in Christ. When this happens the individual is born again and the Holy Spirit enters to reside in them. He then will empower them to live a life that is less and less given to sin. Simply because a person who has trusted Christ as Savior sins it does not mean that they are not saved. Instead, the important point is how they feel about their sin. They need to be truly sorry for their sin and desire to change rather than accepting their sin. Thus, the critical ideas are the desire to change, see the serious nature of sin and to depend on the power of the Holy Spirit to help us live our lives for God. More about this will be discussed as the book progresses.

In the coming chapter we will investigate what Jesus Himself said about repentance. Of course, since Jesus is God come in the flesh what He says is of primary importance. We all need to take special care to live our lives according to what Jesus taught. As stated before, there seems to be something wrong in the world in regards to repentance and when we look at what the Bible, and Jesus in particular, says about this topic we are closer to understanding what the problem is.

CHAPTER 1

JESUS AND REPENTANCE

Of course, due to His status of being God come in the flesh, what Jesus says about any topic is critical. We can look at the pages of Scripture and see how Jesus interacted with the idea of repentance. One of first times that Jesus mentions repent is found in Matthew 4:17. The background of these words is important. In Matthew 3 it is recorded that Jesus is baptized by John. Then in Matthew 4 we are told that Jesus goes into the wilderness to be tempted. Presumably these events happen close together. The next events that Matthew records are about Jesus beginning his preaching ministry. Matthew 4:12-17 reads:

> 12 When Jesus heard that John had been put in prison, he withdrew to Galilee.
>
> 13 Leaving Nazareth, he went and lived in Capernaum, which was by the lake in the area of Zebulun and Naphtali—
>
> 14 to fulfill what was said through the prophet Isaiah:
>
> 15 "Land of Zebulun and land of Naphtali, the Way of the Sea, beyond the Jordan, Galilee of the Gentiles—
>
> 16 the people living in darkness have seen a great light; on those living in the land of the shadow of death a light has dawned."
>
> 17 From that time on Jesus began to preach, "Repent, for the kingdom of heaven has come near."

Directly after this event Matthew records that Jesus begins to call His disciples. Thus, it seems that from the earliest stages of His ministry Jesus preached repentance. It is interesting that Jesus also says to repent for the kingdom of heaven has come near. Jesus is, of course, referring to Himself here. Jesus seems to be saying to those who have not previously repented that it is critically important for them to do it now that He is near.

Later in His earthly ministry Jesus laments the fact that the people in the towns where he taught and did His miracles had refused to repent. Matthew 11:20 states: "Then Jesus began to denounce the towns in which most of his miracles had been performed, because they did not repent." Jesus then goes on to announce woes to these towns that refused repentance. This highlights the importance that Jesus placed on repentance as He was disappointed with those who refused repentance and proclaimed that they would later regret it. The same is true today as all those who refuse to repent, both in changing their mind about Christ and changing their actions, will one day regret it. I think of this in our times as people who are involved in a church, have seen God do miracles, heard the teaching about Jesus and seen the impact a Christian life has on a person and yet still refuse to turn away from their sins in repentance. Jesus spoke about it being worse for the towns in His day that saw His works but did not repent and I cannot help but think it is similar today for those who have been around the work of God but do not repent.

Jesus also presents the idea of repentance when speaking with the Pharisees. As the religious leaders of the day the Pharisees should have known who Jesus was and been His supporters. However, they had their own agenda in life and did not have room for a Messiah that would take away from their power and importance. I suppose this is the heart of everyone who refuses to repent-they have their own agenda in life and do not have room for a Messiah that will change that. As with everyone, Jesus loved the Pharisees and wanted them to repent and believe in Him so he shared this parable with them in Matthew 21:28-32:

__28__ "What do you think? There was a man who had two sons. He went to the first and said, 'Son, go and work today in the vineyard.'

__29__ "'I will not,' he answered, but later he changed his mind and went.

__30__ "Then the father went to the other son and said the same thing. He answered, 'I will, sir,' but he did not go.

__31__ "Which of the two did what his father wanted? "The first," they answered. Jesus said to them, "Truly I tell you, the tax collectors and the prostitutes are entering the kingdom of God ahead of you.

__32__ For John came to you to show you the way of righteousness, and you did not believe him, but the tax collectors and the prostitutes did. And even after you saw this, you did not repent and believe him."

In the parable that Jesus told about the two sons, the first one represents the tax collector's and prostitutes or those who early in their lives said they would not serve God. However, later in life they repented of their sin and were now trying to follow Jesus. The second son represented those who initially said they would follow God but did not. This parable highlights the importance of really following God with all of our hearts rather than simply saying we will follow God and then not doing it. Jesus pointedly tells the religious leaders that they are like the second son because they said they would follow God but they have not followed through with actually doing it. Jesus said that the very ones they thought of as 'sinners' would enter heaven but the Pharisees themselves would not. What was the key difference between these Pharisees and the tax collectors and prostitutes? The tax collectors and prostitutes of Jesus' day had committed sins that most people would think of as worse than anything the Pharisees had done yet. However, the difference lay in that the tax collector's and prostitutes were willing to repent and find forgiveness while the Pharisees were not willing to repent. We can see the importance that Jesus placed on repentance in His interactions with people during His earthly life.

In the book of Luke, Jesus gives us some interesting words to ponder concerning repentance. Apparently, Pilate had killed some Galileans and had mixed their blood with his sacrifices. Some of the people there asked Jesus about this event and Jesus used it as a time of teaching and warning. Luke 13:1-9 tells us:

<u>1</u> Now there were some present at that time who told Jesus about the Galileans whose blood Pilate had mixed with their sacrifices.

<u>2</u> Jesus answered, "Do you think that these Galileans were worse sinners than all the other Galileans because they suffered this way?

<u>3</u> I tell you, no! But unless you repent, you too will all perish.

<u>4</u> Or those eighteen who died when the tower in Siloam fell on them—do you think they were more guilty than all the others living in Jerusalem?

<u>5</u> I tell you, no! But unless you repent, you too will all perish."

<u>6</u> Then he told this parable: "A man had a fig tree growing in his vineyard, and he went to look for fruit on it but did not find any.

<u>7</u> So he said to the man who took care of the vineyard, 'For three years now I've been coming to look for fruit on this fig tree and haven't found any. Cut it down! Why should it use up the soil?'

<u>8</u> 'Sir,' the man replied, 'leave it alone for one more year, and I'll dig around it and fertilize it.

<u>9</u> If it bears fruit next year, fine! If not, then cut it down.' "

Jesus uses current events to teach a lesson. He says that the Galileans that suffered in this way were not worse sinners than everyone else. Rather Jesus tells the crowd that unless they repent that they will also perish.

There was another event at this time as a tower had fallen and killed 18 people. Jesus also says that these 18 were not worse sinners but that all those listening (and reading some 2000 years later) would also perish unless they repented. Another interesting side line from what Jesus said is that tragedy can strike at any time and those who are harmed or killed in this way are not necessarily being punished for their sins. Rather, God knows the days of our lives and at times accidents happen through no fault of our own. As I write this I learned of a terrible event today. Some friends of mine have an 18 year old son. They were all traveling together when something came out of bed of the pickup truck. The young man, as a good son should, got out of the truck to retrieve it and was struck by another vehicle and killed. I cannot imagine the pain the family is feeling right now. This young man was a fine person and was not being punished for some wrong doing. Rather, God is in control and tragedies happen to both the godly and ungodly. If this event had happened in Jesus' day He could have also used it as an example.

Jesus then says the words that would probably get everyone's attention by saying that unless each of the listeners repent they also will perish. From all that we know of Jesus' teachings we understand that He was not talking here about physical death but that He meant an eternal perishing or separation from God in a place called hell. Jesus is trying to get the message to listeners that repenting now is of utmost importance because we never know when a similar tragedy might strike us. As well, Jesus is wanting them to understand that the people who died in these tragedies did not think their lives would soon be over. It was important for these people to have repented of their sin and it is important both for the listeners in Jesus' time and for us also. None of us know when a tragedy will strike our own lives so it is important to repent of our sins and trust in Christ so that we will be prepared. It is also of interest that many of the listeners who refused to repent when they heard the words of Jesus would perish some 30 years later in the fall of Jerusalem to the Romans.

Jesus follows these startling words by sharing a parable that is related to the conversation He was just having. The parable concerns a man looking for fruit on a fig tree. He is disappointed to find no fruit for the third year in a row and contemplates cutting the fig tree down. The caretaker then tells the owner to give the tree one more year. He will tend carefully for the tree and fertilize it. If this special care does not work with the tree still bearing no fruit then it should be cut down.

It appears that at the end of the parable that Jesus is trying to give a warning to all those who refuse to repent. Most specifically it is to the Pharisees as Jesus seems to be telling them that they have heard the truth about the Messiah and that if there is not a change in their lives then they will be removed. This is exactly what happened to most of the Pharisees as very few of them repented of their sin and trusted Christ. Thus, they removed themselves from God's work of spreading the truth of God to the world. This work was then given to the disciples and other early followers of Christ but the Pharisees had been warned.

I believe that this also has application to those of us living today. God has allowed us to hear the message of faith in Christ for forgiveness of sins and yet many people still refuse to repent of their sin and trust Christ. I believe that Jesus is saying that the time for repentance has been extended for each one reading this book. However, that time will soon come to an end for each of us and then those who do not repent will be lost without hope. Now is the time to make our decision to repent and trust in Christ.

JESUS AND THE LOST SHEEP

In the book of Luke Jesus responds to the Pharisees who are concerned that He is spending time with people they considered to be sinners. Of course, it should be noted that the Pharisees thought of these people as sinners because of their outward lifestyle while they failed to see their own inner attitudes as sinful. In Luke 15:1-7 Jesus responds to them in this way:

<u>1</u> Now the tax collectors and sinners were all gathering around to hear Jesus.

<u>2</u> But the Pharisees and the teachers of the law muttered, "This man welcomes sinners and eats with them."

<u>3</u> Then Jesus told them this parable:

<u>4</u> "Suppose one of you has a hundred sheep and loses one of them. Doesn't he leave the ninety-nine in the open country and go after the lost sheep until he finds it?

<u>5</u> And when he finds it, he joyfully puts it on his shoulders

<u>6</u> and goes home. Then he calls his friends and neighbors together and says, 'Rejoice with me; I have found my lost sheep.'

<u>7</u> I tell you that in the same way there will be more rejoicing in heaven over one sinner who repents than over ninety-nine righteous persons who do not need to repent.

This is one of the most touching parables of Jesus as He compares a sinful person coming to Him as a person who goes out pursuing a lost sheep. Although it is only one sheep and there are 99 left in the fold the shepherd goes out searching for the one that is lost. When he finds the lost sheep he joyfully carries him back to the fold and has a celebration. Jesus is comparing this to how He feels when there is a person who has not trusted Him as savior. He pursues them and when He finds them (meaning they are willing to repent of their sin and trust in Christ) He carries them back with great rejoicing. What a beautiful picture of how God feels about each one us! At one point in their lives, every Christian was the one lost sheep that our Heavenly Father went to find and when we trusted in Christ He carried us back and made us a part of His eternal family.

For our purpose in considering repentance it is important to take a closer look at verse 7. Jesus does not say that there is rejoicing in heaven over one sinner that believes, although we know that believing in Christ is a necessary part of salvation. Rather Jesus chooses to say that there is rejoicing in heaven over one sinner that repents. Here Jesus is again emphasizing the idea that a person needs to repent or be willing to turn away from their sin when they trust in Christ. Jesus seems to be saying that there is no valid salvation experience in which the person comes to Christ but has every intention of continuing in their sin. Jesus is coupling believing in Him with being willing to turn away from sin.

It is also of interest to note the audience that is present at this time. First of all, there are those who are known to be sinners themselves and appear to be considering becoming a follower of Jesus. Jesus lets them know in a subtle way that when they come to follow Him it is expected that they repent of their sin. Secondly, we have the religious leaders present to hear this parable. I think Jesus also wanted them to know that both this group that they think of as sinners and themselves will need to repent when they make the decision to follow Christ.

ZACCHAEUS AND REPENTANCE

When I think about a biblical example of repentance one of the first ones that comes to mind is Zacchaeus. In Luke 19:1-10 we read Zacchaeus' story:

<u>1</u> Jesus entered Jericho and was passing through.

<u>2</u> A man was there by the name of Zacchaeus; he was a chief tax collector and was wealthy.

<u>3</u> He wanted to see who Jesus was, but because he was short he could not see over the crowd.

<u>4</u> So he ran ahead and climbed a sycamore-fig tree to see him, since Jesus was coming that way.

<u>5</u> When Jesus reached the spot, he looked up and said to him, "Zacchaeus, come down immediately. I must stay at your house today."

__6__ So he came down at once and welcomed him gladly.

__7__ All the people saw this and began to mutter, "He has gone to be the guest of a sinner."

__8__ But Zacchaeus stood up and said to the Lord, "Look, Lord! Here and now I give half of my possessions to the poor, and if I have cheated anybody out of anything, I will pay back four times the amount."

__9__ Jesus said to him, "Today salvation has come to this house, because this man, too, is a son of Abraham.

__10__ For the Son of Man came to seek and to save the lost."

One of first things to note about Zacchaeus is that he was a tax collector. At that time in history tax collectors were known to be sinful individuals who were not only dishonest but also considered to not be loyal to the Jewish people. They were known for taking extra money from the Jewish people above what the tax was and using this extra money for their own benefit. As well, the tax collectors often grew to be wealthy from their dishonesty and this is the case for Zacchaeus.

However, it seems that Zacchaeus had come to the point in his life where he knew that he needed a change and this is the key. Any person who has been saved or born again must come to the point where they know that they need a change. Zacchaeus had knowledge that Jesus was coming to his town and he wanted to see Him. In Zacchaeus' mind I believe that he was hoping that Jesus could provide the change that he desperately needed.

Zacchaeus was willing to do whatever he needed to do so that he could see Jesus. He was even willing to become undignified and climb up into a tree. An adult man climbing a tree was not something that was seen very often in that culture and would have been considered an undignified way for a wealthy man to act. In addition, Zacchaeus was short and I would guess that there might have been some snickering by the townspeople when they saw him in a tree. However, Zacchaeus did not seem to care what others thought as he understood that he desperately needed a change in his life. Desperately needing a change is also a key to salvation today. When we trust in Christ we need to be desperate for a change and not care about what others might think about us.

When Jesus saw Zacchaeus in the tree He knew that here was a man that wanted a change. Jesus knew, as He still does today, who was wanting something different in their lives and who just wanted to be around Him and the miracles. Zacchaeus was one of those who was desperate for a change and so Jesus called for him to come down. It is interesting at this point to note that Zacchaeus came down immediately to see Jesus. The Bible did not say that he thought about it for a moment or waited but rather that he came down quickly. Zacchaeus was willing to reach out for the change that he needed and he did not need time to think about it. Desperation does that in a person' life.

It would also seem that the townspeople were shocked that Jesus would look up at Zacchaeus and ask him to come down. The people must have thought: 'Why him of all people? He is definitely a sinful man and Jesus has a reputation for being holy. Surely there are other people much more worthy of Jesus spending time with them.' However, what the townspeople could not see was that Zacchaeus had a heart that was willing to change.

At this point in the event something important happened that showed where Zacchaeus' heart truly was. When the people wondered why Jesus would go to the house of a sinner Zacchaeus made a statement that must have shocked the townspeople. Zacchaeus repented of his sin. He told Jesus that he would pay back four times the amount to anyone that he had cheated. This is a huge statement and would make a great impact on the financial status of Zacchaeus. However, he no longer seemed to care. It was important for him to repent of his past wrongs and make a change. In addition, Zacchaeus revealed that money no longer had a hold on him as he was willing to give half of his goods to the poor. Truly, Zacchaeus revealed his heart. Money no longer was the driving force in his life and he was desiring to embrace a new way of living.

Jesus replied to Zacchaeus, and the crowd, with the greatest words that could ever be heard. Jesus has a personal message for him as He tells Zacchaeus that salvation has come to his house. What a happy day that was for Zacchaeus. He had finally gotten the purpose and meaning to his life that he had been missing and that wealth and position could not provide. Jesus also had a message about His purpose in coming for all to hear. His purpose was not to call those who already thought they were righteous but rather to call those who knew they were lost in sin. Hearing what the true purpose of the Messiah coming was not only a happy day for Zacchaeus but all those that heard it, including us these many centuries later.

One of the critical aspects of this event that is often not emphasized is the attitude that Zacchaeus had towards his previous sinful life. This event would have been unimaginable if Zacchaeus had stayed in his previous sinful life of cheating people out of their money. He was not only willing to believe in Jesus and seek a relationship with Him but Zacchaeus also understood that he needed to turn away from his sin. The idea that Zacchaeus is not only willing to believe but also willing to repent of his sin is a crucial element to understanding all that happened to Zacchaeus that day. The same idea is true today. People need to not only be willing to believe in Jesus but they also need to understand that coming to faith in Christ includes a desire to turn away from sin.

A WOMAN CAUGHT IN ADULTERY

Another interesting event concerns the woman caught in adultery. Her story is seen in John 8:2-11:

> 2 At dawn he appeared again in the temple courts, where all the people gathered around him, and he sat down to teach them.
>
> 3 The teachers of the law and the Pharisees brought in a woman caught in adultery. They made her stand before the group
>
> 4 and said to Jesus, "Teacher, this woman was caught in the act of adultery.

5 In the Law Moses commanded us to stone such women. Now what do you say?"

6 They were using this question as a trap, in order to have a basis for accusing him. But Jesus bent down and started to write on the ground with his finger.

7 When they kept on questioning him, he straightened up and said to them, "Let any one of you who is without sin be the first to throw a stone at her."

8 Again he stooped down and wrote on the ground.

9 At this, those who heard began to go away one at a time, the older ones first, until only Jesus was left, with the woman still standing there.

10 Jesus straightened up and asked her, "Woman, where are they? Has no one condemned you?"

11 "No one, sir," she said. "Then neither do I condemn you," Jesus declared. "Go now and leave your life of sin."

In this Scripture Jesus had just sat down to teach the people in the temple courts. Apparently, the Pharisees were aware that Jesus was there teaching and so they brought a situation before Him. It is noteworthy that they were using this as a method to test Jesus rather than wanting to know the correct way of thinking about the situation. The Pharisees desired to lead Jesus into saying something against the law so that they might accuse Him and, also, to put Him in a negative light in front of the crowds. Neither of these goals would be reached but rather a new understanding of sin and punishment for those who were willing to listen.

The Pharisees conveniently had found a woman caught in adultery and so they brought her in and asked Jesus what should be done to her. To increase the embarrassment of the situation she had to stand before the group. At first Jesus would not respond to them but bent down and wrote on the ground. However, the Pharisees and teachers of the law were not willing to let the situation go unanswered and so they continued to press Him for an answer.

The Pharisees and teachers of the law were not being dishonest when they said that the law stated that a person caught in this type of sin should be stoned. This is the punishment that the law prescribed. In a certain way, the woman caught in adultery represents each of us. The Bible states in Romans 3:23: "All have sinned and come short of the glory of God." Every person, except for Jesus, of course, has sinned and broken God's law. The Bible tells us that the wages of our sin is death. Not just physical death but spiritual death as we are separated from God without hope. We are all like this woman in that we deserve to be punished. Jesus is about to step in and do something the Pharisees did not expect and in a way that they definitely did not foresee.

Jesus tells them that the one in their company that is without sin should be the first one to cast a stone. This is also true when we are confronting people about their sin today. When someone is sorry for their sin there is no one that can continue to accuse them because we have all sinned. The Bible does say that a Christian has a responsibility to confront another Christian when they are known to be in sin (Matthew 18:15-17, I Corinthians 5:9-11). However, once an individual has repented of their sin then no one has the right to confront them or bring the sin back up again.

After Jesus told them this He seems to casually bend down and start writing on the ground again. Each of the accusers begins to leave one by one, presumably because they are being reminded of the sin in their own lives. Curiously, the older ones are the first to walk away. Perhaps they have gained some wisdom in their lives and understood they had not led a life without sin.

After all the accusers had left, Jesus then stands again and asks the woman where her accusers are and has no one condemned you. The woman responds that no one is left to accuse her. I am sure that this was a shocking moment for the woman. She was fully expecting to be stoned that day and now Jesus had spoken wise words that caused every accuser to leave.

I believe the woman was astonished and not sure what would happen now. Jesus was completely righteous and so if anyone had the right to punish someone for their sin then He certainly did. However, Jesus simply asked where her accusers were now and she told Him that there was no one left to condemn her. Jesus then said something amazing in that He told her that He did not condemn her either.

In this situation Jesus is presenting a new way of dealing with sin. It was a part of the law to stone someone caught in an open sin. Stoning had been practiced many times. However, Jesus is presenting a new way of viewing it to the crowd He was teaching that day. Jesus introduces a new era of forgiveness. The crowd that heard His words that day must have truly been in awe and somewhat perplexed at the same time.

Jesus then says something to the woman that is often missed. He told her to go now and leave her life of sin. I believe that Jesus saw that this woman was willing to repent and so her offered her mercy. Even in this iconic event from the Bible we can see that forgiveness and repentance were tied together. The woman could do nothing to pay for her past sins and Jesus gave her undeserved mercy. At this same time, Jesus called on the woman to live in His forgiveness by leaving her life of sin. This is always what God desires when He shows mercy. He wants the one who receives that forgiveness to truly repent and leave their life of sin.

REPENTANCE WITH THE RICH MAN AND LAZARUS

In Luke 16 there is the interesting story about the rich man and Lazarus. Many people would consider this to be a parable. However, parables do not generally use the name of the person in the story so there is good reason to believe that this was a real event that Jesus is describing. The basis of the event is that the rich man lived an easy life and apparently had no care about his relationship with God or in helping those in need. Lazarus was a poor man who would lay at the gate of the rich man. The Bible said that Lazarus would have gladly eaten of the crumbs from the table of the rich man but it seems that nothing was offered to him.

In time, both Lazarus and the rich man died. The rich man woke up after death being in torment while Lazarus was with Abraham in paradise. Somehow, and it is not clear if this is a common occurrence, the rich man is able to see Lazarus. First the rich man asks for something for himself as he requests Lazarus to come and bring just one drop of water as he was in torment. His request is refused because he had already made his choices while on the earth. This speaks to us about the reality of being separated from God forever. Once we have made our decisions during our earthly lives there will not be an opportunity to change them later. Next the rich man requests this in Luke 16:27-31:

> <u>27</u> "He answered, 'Then I beg you, father, send Lazarus to my family,
>
> <u>28</u> for I have five brothers. Let him warn them, so that they will not also come to this place of torment.'
>
> <u>29</u> "Abraham replied, 'They have Moses and the Prophets; let them listen to them.'
>
> <u>30</u> "'No, father Abraham,' he said, 'but if someone from the dead goes to them, they will repent.'
>
> <u>31</u> "He said to him, 'If they do not listen to Moses and the Prophets, they will not be convinced even if someone rises from the dead.' "

The rich man is concerned for his five brothers that are still alive. He does not want them to join him in this place of torment. This goes directly against the idea that hell will be a party where people will be able to have fun with their friends. Quite the opposite is true as the rich man wants someone to warn his brothers. Abraham states that they have the prophets and that they can listen to them. The rich man then says a comment that is very interesting in light of what will soon happen to Jesus as He will be raised from the dead. The rich man believes that if someone comes back from the dead to warn his brothers then they will repent. Abraham replies that though someone comes back from the dead that they still will not be convinced. Indeed, Jesus has risen from the dead and yet many people remained unconvinced to become His follower.

The important section of this passage for our purposes is when the rich man says that his brothers will repent and then Abraham says that they will not be convinced. The rich man uses a form of the Greek word metanoia which is the common word for repent in the New Testament.

The rich man seems to understand that in order for his brothers to avoid a place of torment they will need to turn away from their sinful lives. Again, he appears to understand that for his brothers to avoid torment they need to change their beliefs and repent of their sins. Abraham responds with the Greek word peisthesontai. This word is used only once in the New Testament and it is best interpreted as to be persuaded. Thus, Abraham is forwarding the idea that they will need to be persuaded to repent of their sins and believe. The important point for our study is that there is clear evidence that it is required to repent and turn away from sin so that one can avoid eternal punishment and separation from God.

REPENTANCE AND JOHN THE BAPTIST

Now that we have looked at what Jesus said about repentance we should also review what John the Baptist said about the topic. One of the highly esteemed men in the Bible that taught a message of repentance was John the Baptist. John was actually a cousin to Jesus and was born a few months before Him. However, it appears that Jesus and John the Baptist did not see each other during the first 30 years of their lives. They came together for the first time when John was preaching in the wilderness. The ministry of John the Baptist is important because he comes before Jesus and prepares the way for Him. Thus, the message that John is preaching is a part of what Jesus will preach later.

John's message is one of repentance and turning away from sin. Matthew 3:1-12 give us some insight into John's ministry:

<u>1</u> In those days John the Baptist came, preaching in the wilderness of Judea

<u>2</u> and saying, "Repent, for the kingdom of heaven has come near."

<u>3</u> This is he who was spoken of through the prophet Isaiah: "A voice of one calling in the wilderness, 'Prepare the way for the Lord, make straight paths for him.'"

<u>4</u> John's clothes were made of camel's hair, and he had a leather belt around his waist. His food was locusts and wild honey.

<u>5</u> People went out to him from Jerusalem and all Judea and the whole region of the Jordan.

<u>6</u> Confessing their sins, they were baptized by him in the Jordan River.

<u>7</u> But when he saw many of the Pharisees and Sadducees coming to where he was baptizing, he said to them: "You brood of vipers! Who warned you to flee from the coming wrath?

<u>8</u> Produce fruit in keeping with repentance.

<u>9</u> And do not think you can say to yourselves, 'We have Abraham as our father.' I tell you that out of these stones God can raise up children for Abraham.

<u>10</u> The ax is already at the root of the trees, and every tree that does not produce good fruit will be cut down and thrown into the fire.

11 "I baptize you with water for repentance. But after me comes one who is more powerful than I, whose sandals I am not worthy to carry. He will baptize you with the Holy Spirit and fire.

12 His winnowing fork is in his hand, and he will clear his threshing floor, gathering his wheat into the barn and burning up the chaff with unquenchable fire."

There are several things that we should take notice of from this passage of Scripture. The first is that John the Baptist calls for people to repent or turn away from their sin because the kingdom of heaven has come near. Of course, John is referring to the arrival of Jesus. The Bible teaches us that the proper response to Jesus, God come in the flesh, is always to turn away from our sin. It logically follows that since Jesus has come in the flesh and that now God is always near us in the form of the Holy Spirit that our response should always be one of repentance.

The second aspect of this passage that we find interesting is that John tells the Pharisees to produce fruit in keeping with repentance. What does John mean by this? To understand this we should look at the background of the Pharisees. They were religious leaders who specialized in looking good to others on the outside while inside they were filled with sinful attitudes and did not truly have a desire to live for God. They were most interested in fulfilling their own will and keeping their position in society rather than wanting the kingdom of God to come. The Pharisees were the type of people who might want others to believe that they had repented without actually having a change of heart. Therefore, John tells them that they need to truly show that they had repented by a change in their lifestyle. The outward change would be a sign of what had already happened on the inside. This should also be a lesson for us. True repentance will not only be an inward attitude but will also produce outward fruits that others can see.

A third idea that we should understand from this passage is what John says about having Abraham as their father. The Pharisees, as well as many Jewish people of the day, thought that they were somehow automatically right with God because they descended from Abraham. However, John tells them that one must repent of their sin and have true faith in God to be part of the family of God. This is still the same today. An individual must trust in Christ alone for salvation and repent of their sin to be a part of God's family. While the Jews of Jesus' day trusted in their being a descendant of Abraham, today we have different ideas that we cling to for salvation. Some of those include belonging to a church, coming from a Christian family, being baptized, being confirmed or taking communion. All of these are only outward signs of what should have already taken place on the inside. If a person trusts in one of these things without repenting of their sin and trusting in Christ then their fate will be the same as the Pharisees and they will spend an eternity separated from God.

The events of the life of the John the Baptist are also covered in the Gospel of Luke. God leads Luke to share some other details that are of interest in our understanding of repentance. Luke 3:7-14 presents these details:

> 7 John said to the crowds coming out to be baptized by him, "You brood of vipers! Who warned you to flee from the coming wrath?
>
> 8 Produce fruit in keeping with repentance. And do not begin to say to yourselves, 'We have Abraham as our father.' For I tell you that out of these stones God can raise up children for Abraham.
>
> 9 The ax is already at the root of the trees, and every tree that does not produce good fruit will be cut down and thrown into the fire."
>
> 10 "What should we do then?" the crowd asked.

11 John answered, "Anyone who has two shirts should share with the one who has none, and anyone who has food should do the same."

12 Even tax collectors came to be baptized. "Teacher," they asked, "what should we do?"

13 "Don't collect any more than you are required to," he told them.

14 Then some soldiers asked him, "And what should we do?" He replied, "Don't extort money and don't accuse people falsely—be content with your pay."

The crowd is interested in what John means by repentance and so they ask him what they should do. He tells the crowd in general that they should share what they have, whether it be food or clothing. In order words, John is calling upon the people to repent of being selfish. It is interesting that verse 12 says 'even' the tax collectors. The tax collectors were known to be greedy and to cheat people, as we saw with Zacchaeus. The Lord is having Luke make the point that even this outwardly sinful group is desiring to turn to God. John replies by telling them that they should not collect any more than they are required to. This would be a tremendous change for this group because they enjoyed tremendous financial gain from exhorting more taxes and keeping the difference. However, John calls upon them to repent of their sinful actions as Zacchaeus had done. As well, some soldiers want to know what God is asking of them. John gives them three directives in telling them to not extort money, not accuse people falsely and be content with their wages. For the soldiers this would also be a big change for them. John is calling upon them to repent of their previous sins of greed, dishonesty and being ungrateful.

A key point of understanding is that John is saying that if they have really repented and turned to God then this will be followed by a change in their lifestyle. We need to keep this in mind also. Whenever a person has come to true faith in Christ it will result in changes that can soon be seen on the outside. Repentance brings about a turning away from sin and a different way of living.

Thus, when we study the words of Jesus and his predecessor, John the Baptist, we can see that coming to faith in Christ is coupled with repentance from past sinful lifestyles. The idea that a person can come to faith in Christ and have intentions to continue in a life of sin are foreign to the teachings of the Gospels. Later, we will look at the Old Testament and the impact that repentance had on the people living in that time period. Although the belief system was not exactly the same because they were looking forward to the coming of the Messiah, we will see that repentance and faith in the true God were still ideas that went together. Before doing that let's take some time to consider the impacts of sin and God's discipline.

CHAPTER 2

THE IMPACTS OF SIN AND GOD'S DISCIPLINE

Now that we have understood what Jesus said about repentance it is important to consider some of the aspects of sin and repentance before delving deeper into what the Bible teaches in the Old Testament. The primary reason to avoid sin in our lives is because of the negative impact. We need to understand that God takes sin and repentance very seriously. Most importantly, though, we are blessed to know that God disciplines those that become one of His children through faith in Christ and repentance and that He will help every sincere believer by doing the changing necessary. God simply asks us to put our faith in Christ, repent of our sin and be willing to allow Him to change us from the inside.

IMPACTS OF SIN

One of the most important impacts of sin is that it hinders our having a close relationship with God. Unrepentant sin hinders us from having a strong relationship with our Heavenly Father. It is as if something is clogging the pipes of relationship and blessing between ourselves and God. When I pastored in the mountains of North Carolina several of the area residents depended on water that came from a natural water source higher up on the mountain. This water was a source of life for those who depended on it and they could not thrive without this water. Imagine that there was some blockage in the pipe that carried the life-giving water to their homes. The water would still be available in the same quantity but would not be able to reach them. There could not be a solution to the problem until the blockage was removed. Sin that has not been repented of can have a similar impact in the life of the believer. Whenever a Christian has sin in their life that they have not repented of then their relationship with God is hindered. In other words, something is clogging the pipe in our relationship with God and the blessings cannot flow as intended until the sinful action or attitude has been eliminated. Thus, our relationship with God being all that God intended for it to be is dependent upon our being repentant of all known sin. Our relationship with the Lord is too valuable to have it hindered by anything.

CAN REPENTANCE BE PRE-PLANNED

Some years ago I remember watching a reality television program. One of the contestants said that they were a Christian. However, this particular contestant was dishonest several times in order to manipulate other contestants. In an interview on the show they claimed that their dishonesty was not a problem because they could simply approach the other contestant later and apologize and then ask God to forgive them. When they did this they claimed everything would be fine and their sin would not be a problem. What is wrong with this picture?

The problem with the way the contestant approached the situation was that they were presuming upon God's grace. They thought that if they simply asked God to forgive them then that made it ok for them to commit any sin. However, if we intentionally commit a sin and plan on asking God's forgiveness, have we truly repented? Remember that part of repentance is wishing that if we could go back in time and be in the same situation we would do things differently and never commit the sin in the first place. Until we feel that way about a sin then true repentance has not occurred. The misguided reality show contestant could not see this but they were presuming upon God's grace by intentionally committing a sin and then planning to ask forgiveness. With this type of thinking there is never true repentance.

I have heard several people make similar statements through the years. They would say that they were planning to commit a certain sin but that it would be ok because later on they would simply ask God to forgive them. They believed that there would be no harm done. However, we cannot plan to commit sin in this way. There are several problems with this viewpoint. The first, of course, is that we do not recognize the impact of sin on our lives and the lives of others. Sin should never be taken lightly because it can have lasting impacts. Secondly, this way of thinking does not take into account the impact that it will have on our relationship with God. Our relationship with God is too valuable to allow a pre-planned sin to hinder that connection. There are too many sins in our lives that we step into without planning ahead of time to add to that by sinning intentionally. A third problem with this viewpoint is that it does not consider the disdain that a holy God has for sin. Jesus paid a great price on the cross to pay our sin debt. God has such an aversion to sin that He looked away from the His Son when Jesus was paying the sin debt on the cross. When we have a nonchalant attitude about sin we do not recognize how our holy God views sin. Simply knowing how God feels about sin and what Jesus had to suffer to pay for our sins should be enough to try to avoid sin in our lives at all costs rather than embracing the idea of sin by planning to later ask forgiveness.

The lesson we can take from this is that we need to be repentant for our sin. When we plan on sinning and then later presuming upon God's grace then we have not experienced true repentance. When we do not have real repentance then that sin will hinder our relationship with our Heavenly Father. That relationship is the most valuable aspect of our lives and nothing should be worth it to us to hinder it.

THE IMPORTANCE OF GOD'S DISCIPLINE

When we are considering the impacts of sin we need to understand that there are consequences for sin. Discipline is related to repentance. For the Christian, it is God's discipline that brings us to a point of repentance.

In the human realm most of us want to avoid being disciplined, chastised or punished if we can. However, in the spiritual life it is different than in the strictly human realm. We should desire to be disciplined by God when we have sinned. This sounds odd at first but when we think about it in relation to Scripture we should desire God's discipline for sin. Hebrews 12:5-11 tells us:

> <u>5</u> And have you completely forgotten this word of encouragement that addresses you as a father addresses his son? It says, "My son, do not make light of the Lord's discipline, and do not lose heart when he rebukes you,
>
> <u>6</u> because the Lord disciplines the one he loves, and he chastens everyone he accepts as his son."
>
> <u>7</u> Endure hardship as discipline; God is treating you as his children. For what children are not disciplined by their father?
>
> <u>8</u> If you are not disciplined—and everyone undergoes discipline—then you are not legitimate, not true sons and daughters at all.
>
> <u>9</u> Moreover, we have all had human fathers who disciplined us and we respected them for it. How much more should we submit to the Father of spirits and live!
>
> 10 They disciplined us for a little while as they thought best; but God disciplines us for our good, in order that we may share in his holiness.
>
> <u>11</u> No discipline seems pleasant at the time, but painful. Later on, however, it produces a harvest of righteousness and peace for those who have been trained by it.

The writer of Hebrews is inspired of God to open this passage of Scripture about discipline with talking about a word of encouragement. There probably seems to be a disconnect in our thinking between discipline and encouragement but let's look at why God said this.

In verse 5 God tells us to not lose heart when we are disciplined. God created us and knows how we react to things. He knows that at times people can become discouraged when they are chastised. However, God asked us to view it in the exact opposite way. In the next verse God tells us that he disciplines those He loves and that He accepts as His children. Being disciplined by God is a natural aspect of being one of His children. In fact, if we are not disciplined by God when we do wrong then we should be worried. If you can continue in your life breaking one of God's commands or instructions in the Bible and not suffer some negative consequences for it then it is a good sign that you are not truly in the family of God.

Verse 6 even tells us that God disciplines those that He loves. We can also think of this as a natural family. When a father loves his children he wants them to grow up to be respectable citizens and so he disciplines them the best that he knows how to in order so that might become healthy adults both physically and emotionally. The human parent that loves their children does the best they can but they do not always make the best choices because they have limited knowledge. However, our Heavenly Father has perfect knowledge and His discipline is always for our benefit, if we allow it to be, as it will bring us to repentance.

I take a somewhat humorous view of verse 8 when it tells us that 'everyone undergoes discipline.' There are times when Christians begin to think that they live so close to God that they do not get disciplined anymore. Instead, the Bible gives us the clear idea that every Christian will continue to get disciplined until we reach heaven because God is always working with each of us to conform us more and more to the image of Christ. If we ever think that we have arrived and do not need anymore more work then we are probably guilty of pride and God needs to do more molding to rid us of that. We simply need to get used to the idea that God will continue to discipline us for our good so that we can become more and more like Christ. When we have conquered one area in our lives then God begins to mold and shape us in another area that we may not have even thought about before.

As an example of this I think about a man named John Hyde who lived in the late 1800s and early 1900s. He was a missionary and prayer warrior that accomplished much for God's kingdom. After reading his biography and what his friends said about his prayer life he is one of the men that stand out in history for being dedicated to God. I was reading something that he had written about how the Holy Spirit directed his life and it reminds that we will always be on a journey to become more like Christ. John Hyde said that he had been praying for a brother in the faith who was struggling. As we often do, John Hyde reported that he was praying for this brother and mentioning how the man was struggling. He said that suddenly the Holy Spirit impressed upon him that it was wrong for him to say negative things about his brother in his prayers. Instead, John Hyde wrote that the Holy Spirit directed him to recount all the good things that this brother had done in the past and to pray that those good works would continue. Even a great man of God like John Hyde still needed to be disciplined and grow more Christ like so we can surely know that the journey will never end. God will continue to bring new areas into our lives and discipline us to repentance so that we are conformed to the image of Christ.

In verse 11 God tells us that no discipline seems pleasant at the time, but rather, painful. We should want to avoid God's discipline whenever possible but also remember that there will be times when it occurs for everyone and that it is a sign of God's love. We should also be encouraged by knowing that the Bible tells us that the ultimate products of God's discipline are righteousness and peace. As Christians it should be our goal to want to become righteous or as much like Christ as possible. It is beneficial to know that discipline leads us closer and closer to this goal. It is also interesting to note that God also says that discipline results in peace. In our minds undergoing discipline and peace do not normally go hand in hand. However, God's economy is different from our way of thinking and when He disciplines it leads to peace. When we think about it sin in our lives brings about strife, pain and confusion. When we are disciplined by God, if we choose to obey, then the sin that brings strife, pain and confusion is eliminated. When we live a lifestyle of heeding God's discipline and repenting it leads to a life of righteousness and peace.

When I think about this topic and the desire to avoid God's discipline I think of an event in my life. I recently taught a Vacation Bible School. Some of the children could get pretty rowdy at times and it was hard to handle them. Nothing that I told them seemed to work because they sensed that I had no real authority. However, when I mentioned to one of the children that I was going to tell their father how they were misbehaving a shocked and frightened look came on their face. They knew that how they were acting was wrong and that it would displease their parents. They did not want to suffer the consequences of their father finding out and using discipline in their lives. They knew that their father had the true authority to give a just punishment. It should be the same way when we think about our Heavenly Father knowing when we are being disobedient. We should have a healthy fear of God when we are doing wrong. The Word of God tells us in Proverbs 9:10: "The fear of the Lord is the beginning of wisdom, and knowledge of the Holy One is understanding." At the same time we need to understand that God will discipline us to our benefit so that we may become more of the person that He desires us to be.

When God disciplines us, what response is He wanting from us? God desires for us to repent and turn away from our sin. He does not want us to only be sorry for our sin but also to repent and turn away from it. I remember a time when I was a young adult. A couple of friends and I would get together occasionally and would engage in an activity that we knew was wrong. Several times God spoke to me about it but I continued engaging in it. Afterwards I would be sorry and ask for forgiveness but I did not truly repent because I did not intend to stop the activity. Then there was this one time when the three of us were together and we did it again. I immediately felt God's displeasure and I knew that this time discipline was coming. Each one of us as children of God are unique and each of us have a different type of discipline that works best with us based on our personalities and background. God created us and He knows what will best get our attention as His children. At that time in my life the best type of discipline for me was to not feel God's presence in my life. It was a horrible couple of days as I did not feel close to God. At the same time I knew that I undergoing His discipline for a sinful action that I had been warned about. After a short time, and God knows just how long it needs to be, the time of discipline was over and I felt close to God once again. What were the results in my life? Well, I have never engaged in that activity again due to God's grace and help. Next time I was with those friends I steered us away from that and after a short time they also began to see our sinful error for ever allowing that to be a part of our lives. We need to remember that God disciplines every child of His and if you never experience that discipline then you need to be concerned about your salvation.

At times, God's discipline is milder when just a gentle reminder is all that is needed to get us back on track. First let me start by saying, that the Bible tells us in Titus 3:2: "Speak evil of no man, to be no brawlers, but gentle, shewing all meekness unto all men." (KJV) That phrase 'Speak evil of no man…' stands out to me and I believe that God is telling us that we need to not engage in saying negative things about people even if what we are saying is true. I have found that this is one of the hardest commandments to keep. I remember a time several years back when I attended a big revival in another state. A couple of weeks before attending I had knowledge of a pastor who was struggling and making some bad choices in how he engaged with his congregation. I was with a group of people and they were talking negatively about this pastor. Unfortunately, I joined in with them and made some negative comments of my own about this pastor and friend. Well, as God's providence would have it, who do you think I ended up sitting next in this huge revival?

That's right, I was sitting next to the pastor that I had spoken negatively about just a few weeks before. When I hugged him and told him I loved him I felt that little nudge by the Holy Spirit. It was as if the Holy Spirit was saying: "Were you showing love to your brother when you spoke critically of him a few weeks ago." It is easy to say we love people but much harder to live that out in all circumstances. That little nudge was all I needed at that time to truly repent and regret what I had said about him. A similar situation happened with a relative. I had spoken negatively about them and then a few days later who did I run into at a restaurant? Of course, I saw that relative that I rarely see. As I hugging them I again felt the nudge of the Holy Spirit asking if I showed love to them a few days before when I made those negative comments. That nudge was what I needed in both of those instances. However, I firmly believe that if I had persisted in disobeying God without repentance then the discipline would have become more severe.

The point I want us to think about is that God disciplines us for our good and to make us more like Christ. God knows each of His children and He knows the type and severity of discipline that we need in every situation. God's goal in discipline is to bring us to the point of repentance. God wants to mold us into the image of Christ as much as is possible in this life.

GOD DOES THE CHANGING

One of the most important points when it comes to repentance is to understand the role that God has. God does not ask us to do all the changing on our own. He only asks us to come to Him with a willing and repentant heart and He will make the necessary changes. When God changes us it has a lasting impact because He changes our heart and our desires. If you are struggling with sin continuously then perhaps you have been trying to do it on your own without depending on God and the power of a changed life. When a person puts their trust in Christ and His finished work on the cross then God makes them a new person.

II Corinthians 5:17 tells us: "Therefore, if anyone is in Christ, he is a new creation; the old has passed away, and see, the new has come!" The change that God makes gives us power to live for Him.

We have all heard of people wanting to turn over a new leaf and perhaps we have tried to do that ourselves a few times. However, turning over a new leaf will not work because we are trying to do it in our power. It takes a heart that is changed by Christ in order to make a lasting change in our lives. Even if we could be successful and turn over a new leaf it would not make an eternal change. If a person could be successful in living a better life and avoiding sin, they still have the problem of how their sins are going to be paid for. No amount of clean living can ever pay for our sin. It takes a person falling on the mercy of God by trusting in Christ for there to be forgiveness and eternal life.

So, if you are reading this book and struggling with sin that you cannot overcome, take heart because when we trust in Christ and His power then He will do the changing from the inside. He gives us a new heart that desires to live for Him. Stop depending on yourself and your willpower and turn to Christ. He has the power to change the most stubborn and sinful heart into one that will glorify Him.

CHAPTER 3

REPENTANCE IN THE OLD TESTAMENT

Now that we have looked at what Jesus and John the Baptist had to say about Repentance and have considered the impact of sin and God's discipline, we will look at repentance in the Old Testament. Repentance in the Old Testament is represented by a change in mindset. At certain points in the Old Testament there is also emotionalism which is often mistaken for repentance. Of course, emotionalism is true of any time period but we will try to understand it at this point in the lens of the Old Testament. The difference between emotionalism and true repentance is that with emotionalism there is no true desire to change. Repentance in the Old Testament meant not only a sorrow for sin but also a desire to alter the mindset so that sin will be avoided in the future. In fact, the Hebrew word for repent in the Old Testament is most often translated in English as 'turn.' Thus, we can be sure that in the Old Testament repentance was not simply a sorrow for sin (or emotionalism) but, even more importantly, a turning away from sin. As well, wanting to turn away from sin would be the best indication that someone is sorrowful. It does not appear plausible that an individual is truly sorry for sin if there is no desire to change. We can look at this idea relation to Jacob's family.

REPENTANCE IN JACOB'S FAMILY

Jacob was a man that made many mistakes and committed many sins in his life as recorded in the book of Genesis. One of the most prominent ones was his desire to get the birthright of the first born and to do anything necessary to get it. One of Jacob's greatest errors in this area was in not understanding that God had already said that he would eventually receive the benefits of the first born. Jacob was going to get those benefits and there would be no problems if he just trusted God. However, Jacob refused to trust God's timing and so he tried to use manipulation and dishonesty to create a situation where he would get the birthright. All his efforts only led to heartache in his life. This is something we must also be careful about. God has a plan for each of our lives. At times, however, we do not want to be patient and wait for God's timing and so we try to manipulate situations to our advantage. What this truly shows is a lack of faith in God's timing, His goodness towards us and, often, even His ability to bring the events to pass that we think are needed in order to 'move ahead' in our lives. Whenever we take the route of trying to force situations beyond God's timing then it will lead to heartache and the consequences of sin for us.

Jacob seemed to have gotten all these impatient and difficult times behind him and had some wonderful experiences with God. However, later in his life God desired for Jacob to be in Bethel but he took the family to Shechem. The family experienced great tragedy in Shechem. The full story can be found in Genesis 34 but a synopsis of the situation will be given here. Jacob had a daughter named Dinah and she went out to be with the other women of the land. While she was out in the town a man saw her and molested her. Two of her brothers were infuriated and endeavored to take justice into their own hands instead of depending on God. The two brothers, Simeon and Levi, deceived the men of Shechem and slaughtered all of them. To make matters worse, Simeon and Levi did not seem to see anything wrong with what they had done and did not have any desire to repent.

This is the situation that Jacob and his family find themselves in at the opening of Genesis 35. Additionally, it seems that the family had began to heavily worship idols during their time in Shechem. If Jacob is going to preserve his family he needed to make a move as the leader to get back on track. This can only be done by repenting of their sin and returning to where God desired for them to be, Bethel. If you are the leader of your family or group you may need to make similar movements when you see that your family or group has begun to veer from the correct path. God has placed you as a leader for a reason. He has entrusted you with guiding your family or group. When you see them heading in the wrong direction make the correct move of repentance and guide them back to God's path. We can see how Jacob led his family in this dark time in Genesis 35:1-7:

> 1 Then God said to Jacob, "Go up to Bethel and settle there, and build an altar there to God, who appeared to you when you were fleeing from your brother Esau."
>
> 2 So Jacob said to his household and to all who were with him, "Get rid of the foreign gods you have with you, and purify yourselves and change your clothes.
>
> 3 Then come, let us go up to Bethel, where I will build an altar to God, who answered me in the day of my distress and who has been with me wherever I have gone."
>
> 4 So they gave Jacob all the foreign gods they had and the rings in their ears, and Jacob buried them under the oak at Shechem.
>
> 5 Then they set out, and the terror of God fell on the towns all around them so that no one pursued them.
>
> 6 Jacob and all the people with him came to Luz (that is, Bethel) in the land of Canaan.
>
> 7 There he built an altar, and he called the place El Bethel, because it was there that God revealed himself to him when he was fleeing from his brother.

In verse 1 God calls upon Jacob to repent and return to Bethel. Bethel here represents a place and time in Jacob's life when he was living in obedience to God and, subsequently, experiencing God's presence and a close relationship with Him. Jacob responds by telling all of his household to throw away their idols, purify themselves and even put on new clothing to signify the change. Although the word repent is not used in the passage this is what Jacob is instructing his family to do. He is realizing the negative impact that living in Shechem has had on his family and he is calling upon them to turn, or repent, of their sinful ways.

The family seems to accept Jacob's words and desire for repentance as they give all of their idols and other pagan symbols to Jacob and he buries them under a tree. He then also directs them to leave the place that has had such a negative impact on the family and make a physical journey to Bethel. When we see a need for repentance in our lives we sometimes only need to make a mental and spiritual change but there are also times when we need to have a physical change of location. There are times when we find ourselves in a place that is leading us into sinful thoughts and habits. In these circumstances we need to make an alteration in our location in order for repentance to be established.

The events of verse 5 might be confusing until we remember what had previously taken place. Simeon and Levi had been responsible for killing all of the men in Shechem and it is logical to think that the men in the surrounding towns would want to exact revenge on the small family. However, God intervenes on the behalf of Jacob's family and strikes terror into the hearts of the surrounding people so that they would not pursue them. When we are willing to repent God will establish whatever situation is necessary for that to happen. In this circumstance he intervened with physical protection and he does it in various ways for repentant people today.

When the journey is completed and they are back in Bethel they seal their repentance by building an altar there. This symbolizes Jacob and his family's desire to repent and get their lives headed in a godly direction. The important point for us in regards to repentance is that Jacob found himself and those he led in a place, both physically and spiritually, far away from God. He then makes the necessary moves to repent through both physical turning and spiritual change. When we find ourselves in a place far removed from God we must determine to not only be sorry for the situation in which we find ourselves but also to make the necessary changes.

THE BROTHERS NEED FOR MORE REPENTANCE

After the situation that happened to Jacob's family one would think that they had learned something from it and would remain in good fellowship with the Lord. However, as is often the case in our lives, the sons of Jacob found themselves in another situation that would require God's intervention to get them back on track spiritually.

It all started with Jacob showing favoritism within the family. Jacob had a life that was often confusing and so he ended up having children by four different women. However, there was one that was special to him and that he loved her far above the others, Rachel. Jacob and Rachel had two sons who were named Joseph and Benjamin. Rachel died in child birth while having Benjamin. This left Jacob devasted and he clung to Joseph and Benjamin. He preferred these two sons above all the others.

Jacob not only favored Joseph and Benjamin but he made the awful error of making this clear to the rest of the family. As would be expected the older 10 sons became jealous of Joseph. Whenever we favor one person over another it will have negative consequences. God stated that He does not show favoritism and he expects us to follow His example.

The ten older brothers were out in the wilderness tending sheep and Jacob sent his favored son, Joseph, to check on them. There was already animosity between the older sons and Joseph because Joseph had dreams in which he ruled over the rest of the family and his father seemed to treat him as sort of a supervisor over the others. When they saw Joseph coming they saw their chance to eliminate him. They made up a plan to kill him and tell their father that he had been mauled by an animal. However, the eldest son, Reuben, encouraged his brothers to not kill him but leave him in a pit to die. Reuben had his own plan of going back and getting Joseph out of the pit and sparing his life. Unfortunately, the other brothers saw a band of traders coming and so they sold Joseph into slavery hoping to never see or be bothered by him again. The brothers returned to Jacob and told him that his son Joseph had been killed by a wild animal. They did not seem to care how their father would be devasted by this news. Their not caring about the impact on the father revealed just how callous they were about the feelings of others including both Joseph and their father. God was not pleased with this and He was going to create a situation that would bring the brothers to a point of repentance for their horrible act.

Meanwhile, God was with Joseph in Egypt and, through a wonderful divine plan, Joseph rose to being second in command in Egypt with only the Pharoah being more powerful than him. God had also given Joseph knowledge through a dream about a famine that would devastate both Egypt and Canaan, where Joseph's family was residing. The famine would be the means by which God would bring the brothers to repentance. God will often use negative circumstances to bring a person to repentance. In His ultimate wisdom God knows that repentance from sin is more important than any earthly hardship a person might face.

God had given Joseph the wisdom to store food enough to last until the 7-year famine was over. Of course, Jacob's family ran out of food and heard that there was help in Egypt. Through a series of events orchestrated by God, with Joseph's aid, the brothers found themselves in front of Joseph, although they did not realize who he was, with the younger favored son, Benjamin, facing the prospect of staying in Egypt and never seeing his father or family again. This is where we see how God had brought Joseph's brothers to a point of repentance. Genesis 44:18-34 tells us these details as the fourth oldest brother, Judah, is speaking:

18 Then Judah went up to him and said: "Pardon your servant, my lord, let me speak a word to my lord. Do not be angry with your servant, though you are equal to Pharaoh himself.

19 My lord asked his servants, 'Do you have a father or a brother?'

20 And we answered, 'We have an aged father, and there is a young son born to him in his old age. His brother is dead, and he is the only one of his mother's sons left, and his father loves him.'

21 "Then you said to your servants, 'Bring him down to me so I can see him for myself.'

22 And we said to my lord, 'The boy cannot leave his father; if he leaves him, his father will die.'

23 But you told your servants, 'Unless your youngest brother comes down with you, you will not see my face again.'

24 When we went back to your servant my father, we told him what my lord had said.

25 "Then our father said, 'Go back and buy a little more food.'

26 But we said, 'We cannot go down. Only if our youngest brother is with us will we go. We cannot see the man's face unless our youngest brother is with us.'

27 "Your servant my father said to us, 'You know that my wife bore me two sons.

28 One of them went away from me, and I said, "He has surely been torn to pieces." And I have not seen him since.

29 If you take this one from me too and harm comes to him, you will bring my gray head down to the grave in misery.'

30 "So now, if the boy is not with us when I go back to your servant my father, and if my father, whose life is closely bound up with the boy's life,

31 sees that the boy isn't there, he will die. Your servants will bring the gray head of our father down to the grave in sorrow.

32 Your servant guaranteed the boy's safety to my father. I said, 'If I do not bring him back to you, I will bear the blame before you, my father, all my life!'

33 "Now then, please let your servant remain here as my lord's slave in place of the boy, and let the boy return with his brothers.

34 How can I go back to my father if the boy is not with me?

No! Do not let me see the misery that would come on my father."

This passage shows us the culmination of how Judah's, and presumably the other brothers as well, thinking had changed. Judah is quoted here as speaking to his brother Joseph, whose identity is hidden from them. Notice how that in the case of Joseph the brothers did not care about the emotional pain their father felt with the knowledge, albeit false, of his son Joseph's death. It would have been easy for the brothers to leave Benjamin in Egypt and be rid of the second favored son. However, they had experienced a change of heart. Now Judah states that they do not want to bring back word that their father will never see his second favored son, Benjamin, return to him. They are concerned about their father's emotional well-being and do not want him to brought to his death with sorrow. Judah even goes to the point of saying that he will trade places with Benjamin and take his place in captivity in Egypt. This would be a huge sacrifice for Judah as he now had a family of his own back at home.

What a change in attitude! Judah is willing to give up his own freedom and family so that his brother Benjamin can be free. This is a great contrast to how they sold Joseph into slavery and did not seem to care that it would cause their father great sorrow. Judah definitely shows signs here that he has repented of his past wrong towards Joseph and is willing to sacrifice himself rather than have the same thing happen to Benjamin.

This is what repentance is all about. When repentance occurs we are sorry for our actions, would desire to change past wrongs and want to avoid committing future sin. Judah, and it seems to also be true of the other brothers, has revealed all of the earmarks of true repentance. When we think about our past sins we need to ask ourselves if we are truly sorry, would change the past errors if we could and want to avoid committing the same type of sin in the future. This is the essence of true repentance.

ESAU: SEEKING REPENTANCE BUT NOT FINDING IT

An interesting individual from the Bible as it relates to repentance is Esau. Esau was Jacob's twin brother and the child of Isaac and Rebekah. When the twins were born Esau was first which meant he should have received all the benefits at his birth. However, this was not the case. Even while the two children were in Rebekah's womb they were battling one another. Rebekah went to the Lord to ask why this was happening and He replied in Genesis 25:23: "The Lord said to her, 'Two nations are in your womb, and two people from within you will be separated; one people will be stronger than the other, and the older will serve the younger.'" This, of course, would be somewhat surprising news to Rebekah as this was not the normal course of family life at the time. However, in later years Rebekah would come to favor the younger son, Jacob, so this prophecy about him would please her.

Jacob and Esau were very different when they grew up. Esau was a hunter and enjoyed the open country while Jacob preferred to live his life among the tents. There was conflict between the two even at the moment of birth as Jacob grasped onto Esau's heel. Their parents intensified the rivalry as Isaac favored Esau and Rebekah, as mentioned earlier, came to be partial to Jacob. The first big moment in their rivalry came when Esau was very hungry after returning from a hunting trip and Jacob was cooking some stew. Esau asked for some of the stew. Now, Jacob should have willingly given him some of the stew out of brotherly love or at least common human decency, but he was shrewd and saw an opportunity.

Jacob told Esau he would only give him the food if Esau would sell him his birthright. Of course, it is ridiculous to think of trading something as valuable as a birthright for one meal but this is exactly what Esau was willing to do. Esau reasoned that if he was about to die then what good would the birthright be to him anyway. Esau is guilty here of exaggerating his need for food. Many people have been led astray throughout history when they overestimated their need and desire for something that they could obtain immediately. The Bible gives the final word of the scene by stating in Genesis 25:34 that Esau '…despised his birthright.'

It is interesting to investigate what the idea of selling one's birthright might have meant at the time. The birthright had a strong connection to one's spiritual heritage. Therefore, when Esau was willing to give up his birthright so easily it indicated that his spiritual heritage meant very little to him. Esau rather concentrated his attention on material things instead of the spiritual and this seems to be carried out in the rest of his life. God even inspired a New Testament writer to speak of Esau's character as Hebrews 12:16 tells us: "See that no one is sexually immoral, or is godless like Esau, who for a single meal sold his inheritance rights as the oldest son." Thus, Esau had a reputation for being sexually immoral and godless. When Esau 'despised' his birthright he was despising his spiritual heritage and revealing himself to be godless.

When we think about how easily Esau was willing to sell his spiritual heritage for something so trivial as a single meal we can also see that this often happens today. The Bible describes some of the spiritual blessings of a relationship with God through Jesus as being adoption into God's family, forgiveness of sins, complete acceptance by God in Jesus, being freed from the slavery of sin, having the Holy Spirit as our indwelling comforter and guide and having eternal life. All of these are the spiritual heritage of those who trust in Christ. Yet people today give up all these spiritual blessings for momentary 'pleasures' that this world offers. There are many people today that trade their potential spiritual blessings for such things as sexual immorality, bitterness, greed, unforgiveness and addictions just to name a few. Perhaps we are not so different from Esau after all.

The saga of Jacob and Esau continued when their father, Isaac, was ill. Jacob and Rebekah developed a plan in which Jacob would receive the blessing that Isaac intended to give to Esau. Of course, all this scheming was unnecessary as God had already proclaimed that Jacob would take the place of the older son. As mentioned earlier, if they had only waited for God's timing, Jacob and Rebekah could have prevented much suffering and hardship but for now we are focusing on Esau. The plan was for Jacob to bring his father meat while Esau was out hunting. This also included some shenanigans of Jacob dressing in animal skins. They were successful in deceiving Isaac as he believed Jacob was his favorite son Esau and bestowed the blessing on him. When Esau returned from hunting with his food for his father it was quite a scene. Both Isaac and Esau realized what Jacob had done.

At this point, Esau is keenly desirous of some type of blessing from his father. He seems to realize that the blessing of the oldest son has been taken through trickery but he has a strong need to at least receive something from his father. The Bible recounts the event that transpired in Genesis 27:34-38:

34 When Esau heard his father's words, he burst out with a loud and bitter cry and said to his father, "Bless me—me too, my father!"

35 But he said, "Your brother came deceitfully and took your blessing."

36 Esau said, "Isn't he rightly named Jacob? This is the second time he has taken advantage of me: He took my birthright, and now he's taken my blessing!" Then he asked, "Haven't you reserved any blessing for me?"

37 Isaac answered Esau, "I have made him lord over you and have made all his relatives his servants, and I have sustained him with grain and new wine. So what can I possibly do for you, my son?"

38 Esau said to his father, "Do you have only one blessing, my father? Bless me too, my father!" Then Esau wept aloud.

Although God had decided that Jacob would receive the blessings of the older son and Jacob had used deception, the plight of Esau was, at least in part, his own fault. He was the one that had chosen to live a godless life of sexual immorality and ignoring spiritual aspects of his life. It seems that at this point Esau begins to understand something of what his actions will cost him. However, Esau focuses his attention outwardly rather than on his own need for repentance as Genesis 27:41 reads: "Esau held a grudge against Jacob because of the blessings his father had given him. He said to himself, 'The days of mourning for my father are near, then I will kill my brother Jacob.'" With this thought Esau takes an even darker path as he is not only sexually immoral and uninterested in spiritual things but he desires to commit murder.

Thankfully, these plans never come to fruition as Rebekah somehow hears of Esau's plan and encourages Jacob to leave. Many years later Esau and Jacob meet again. By this time both men have done well in life and are able to offer expensive gifts to one another. It is a tense moment for Jacob but Esau does not seek to do him any harm at this later stage in their lives. The Bible records this of their meeting in Genesis 33:3-4: "He himself went on ahead and bowed down to the ground seven times as he approached his brother. But Esau ran to meet Jacob and embrace him, he threw his arms around his neck and kissed him. And they wept."

It is wonderful to understand that the two brothers had this moment together after years of bitterness. What we are most interested in here is the aspect of Esau repenting. The Bible speaks centuries later about what was happening inside Esau in Hebrews 12:17: "For ye know that afterward, when he would have inherited the blessing, he was rejected: for he found no place of repentance, though he sought it carefully with tears." How is it possible for Esau to find no place of repentance and yet to seek it with tears? It seems that Esau regretted the consequences to what he had done because it cost him dearly. However, it does not appear that Esau actually wanted to change. We need to remember that true repentance is not only being sorry for our sin but also having a desire to change whatever we are doing that is displeasing to God. There is no indication that Esau truly saw the horror of his sin and wished that he could go back and change his past. He may have wished he could change the moment that he sold his birthright for a meal or that he left his father to go hunting without anyone to stop Jacob from pretending to be him but there is no indication that Esau truly understood the magnitude of his sinful lifestyle and wished to change to become more pleasing to God. Thus, it is possible today for people to be sorry for the predicament that their sin has created without having a desire to change the overall pattern of selfishness and disobedience to God that is the design of their lives.

REPENTANCE AND EMOTION

Let's further investigate the idea of repentance and emotion by looking at the life of Pharoah. As noted before, repentance is more than emotion. Although at the same time there is often emotion when repentance has taken place. When we are merely emotional about our sin with no desire to change then this results in no lasting change. Being emotional about our sin without a true desire to change leads to false repentance and if someone is going to falsely repent then they might as well continue in their sinful path. Pharoah exemplifies this.

Pharoah is a good example from the Bible of someone who seemed to be driven by emotion and desiring the pain to stop. We come to know about Pharoah's story in the book of Exodus. The children of Israel had been in Egypt for hundreds of years. In the beginning, their time in Egypt was positive for the Israelites as Joseph, as previously mentioned, was second in command to the Pharoah and, hence, they were treated well. However, in time Joseph passed from the scene and the new leaders of Egypt did not remember all of the positives that Joseph had brought to the kingdom. Instead, they began to see the Israelites as a threat because they were growing in number and prospering. The leaders of Egypt decided that they needed to make moves to suppress the children of Israel so over time they began to make their lives more difficult. God was with the Israelites and so nothing the Egyptians did seemed to hinder the growth of the people. The Egyptians responded with ever harsher treatment until the Israelites cried out to God for deliverance. God sent Moses to be His spokesman and lead in the deliverance of the Israelites. However, one big problem stood in the way and his name was Pharoah. He had no intention of allowing the Israelites to leave Egypt and so God had to begin to convince him.

The convincing that God sent was in the form of plagues. Each one of the plagues was meant to reveal the power of the one true God and the futility of going against His wishes. The first plague of changing the water into blood seemed to have no impact on Pharoah. However, the second plague was more effective in getting his attention. Exodus 8: 6-15 reads:

6 So Aaron stretched out his hand over the waters of Egypt, and the frogs came up and covered the land.

7 But the magicians did the same things by their secret arts; they also made frogs come up on the land of Egypt.

8 Pharaoh summoned Moses and Aaron and said, "Pray to the LORD to take the frogs away from me and my people, and I will let your people go to offer sacrifices to the LORD."

9 Moses said to Pharaoh, "I leave to you the honor of setting the time for me to pray for you and your officials and your people that you and your houses may be rid of the frogs, except for those that remain in the Nile."

10 "Tomorrow," Pharaoh said. Moses replied, "It will be as you say, so that you may know there is no one like the LORD our God.

11 The frogs will leave you and your houses, your officials and your people; they will remain only in the Nile."

12 After Moses and Aaron left Pharaoh, Moses cried out to the LORD about the frogs he had brought on Pharaoh.

13 And the LORD did what Moses asked. The frogs died in the houses, in the courtyards and in the fields.

14 They were piled into heaps, and the land reeked of them.

15 But when Pharaoh saw that there was relief, he hardened his heart and would not listen to Moses and Aaron, just as the LORD had said.

In verse 8, after the impact of the second plague had been felt, Pharoah says that if the frogs are taken away then he will allow the Israelites to go and do their sacrifice to God. The Lord did as Pharoah had asked and all of the frogs died except for the ones in the Nile river. However, when Pharoah understood that there was relief from the plague he went back on his commitment and refused to allow the children of Israel to leave.

Imagine the audacity of Pharoah to tell the Lord that he is going to repent of something and then not do it. However, both Christians and non-Christians do the same thing today. I am reminded of a close friend that I worked with years ago. We will call him Joe for this example. Joe was a Christian and genuinely seemed to be interested in following God and growing in his spiritual life. We would often have long discussions about the Lord and the Bible in our free time at work. We worked the midnight shift in a factory and at that time I was leading a Bible study at an assisted living home on Tuesday mornings after I got off work. I would often have the sermon I was going to preach on my mind during work and so Joe would ask me about the topic of the sermon from time to time. One night Joe asked me what I was preaching about the next morning and it had an impact on him. After 20 something years I do not remember the entire topic of the sermon but I do remember the verse that had the impact. I Peter 5:8 states: "Be alert and of sober mind. Your enemy the devil prowls around like a roaring lion looking for someone to devour." Joe told me that he had been struggling with the idea of using a certain drug for recreational purposes. He did not really need the drug but he took it to relax and calm himself down. He had been praying earlier that day about whether or not it was God's will for him to continue to use the recreational drug. He had prayed that if God did not want him to continue to take it that I would say something at work that would discourage him from it. That is a very specific prayer request and God had given him a specific answer. Before that night we had never discussed that drug and I did not know that he indulged in it. Joe told that when I shared the verse about being of a sober mind that he felt like it was a direct answer from God that he should not continue to use that drug. God has the power to answer us specifically when He desires to and He had done that for Joe. Joe expressed his desire to follow God in abandoning his drug use. Now here is the kicker. A few months later I casually asked Joe one night if he was still using that drug. He had a dejected look on his face and said that he was still using it. Even after God had miraculously given him a specific answer to his inquiry, he said that he would repent of it but in the end he did not. Sometimes we look back in amazement at someone like Pharoah who denied God's specific instructions even when God had made it crystal clear. However, we often are guilty of the same type of action. If God has called you to repent and change from something specific it is best to make that change, depending on God's power, before there are dire consequences.

Repentance is more the idea of changing our attitude toward God and also towards sin. When we repent we are really agreeing with God about our sinful past and, also, agreeing with Him that there needs to be a change in the future. The essence is a willingness to change and also to allow God to change us. If we depend only on our own strength to change then we will be unsuccessful. However, when we understand that God can give us the power to change that comes from a new heart and depend upon Him to make the change then we can enjoy success in our endeavors to alter our lives and live for God.

Now, back to our following Pharoah and his actions. The next two plagues were of gnats and flies. Apparently, the plague of flies were too much for Pharoah and he asked Moses to pray for him that the plague of flies would vanish and then he would allow the people to leave. However, after the plague is over Pharoah again hardens his heart and will not let the Israelites leave.

God next sent a plague on the livestock of the Egyptians so that they all died. It is noteworthy that these plagues did not impact the Israelites so that none of their cattle died. At this point, it would seem that Pharoah should have had an alteration in his view as the previous plagues had been inconvenient but now animals were dying. This would be a foreshadowing of a future event. In spite of this, Pharoah would not change his stance.

The next plague of boils did not produce any results. However, when God sent a plague of hail that killed every growing thing in the fields, as well as people and livestock left in the fields, then Pharoah once again said he would change. The Bible states in Exodus 9:27-28: "Then Pharoah summoned Moses and Aaron. 'This time I have sinned,' he said to them. 'The Lord is in the right, and I and my people are in the wrong. Pray to the Lord, for we have had enough thunder and hail. I will let you go; you don't have to stay any longer.'" It is interesting that Pharoah says that he has sinned and that he refers to the God of the Israelites as Lord. We might think that it is amazing that someone knows they are sinning against the Lord and still refuses to truly repent. However, when we think of the example of my friend Joe, and often in our own lives, we see that it is not all that amazing after all but, unfortunately, it is an all too common event to knowingly commit sin against the Lord. As is the expected pattern, Pharoah changes his mind and does not allow the Israelites to leave.

In Exodus 10 God sends Moses to announce the next plague of locusts to Pharoah. It is of interest that the officials of Egypt are now convinced that it is foolish to try and keep the children of Israel from worshipping as verse 7 tells us: "Pharoah's officials said to him, 'How long will this man be a snare to us? Let the people go, so that they may worship the Lord their God. Do you not yet realize that Egypt is ruined?'" However, Pharoah once again refuses but this time on the technicality that he will allow only the men to go but not the women and children. After the plague has been unleashed Pharoah once again follows his old pattern of asking for forgiveness but then refusing to let the people leave. Pharoah is definitely showing a familiar pattern in the type of repentance many people practice. They turn to God in difficult times but then when the suffering is relieved they return back to the their old pattern and forget the promises made to God. Whenever we follow the pattern of making a commitment to God and not following through with it, we are in dangerous territory.

The actions of Pharoah in this case reminds me of what happened to a friend of mine that we will call Jerry. Jerry had been going along in his normal life pattern for years. He was a pretty good guy and claimed to be a Christian. However, Jerry rarely, if ever, went to church and allowed some sinful activities into his life. His life came to a crisis point when he was struck with an anxiety related illness. We talked and prayed during the illness and he said that if God allowed him to pull through this that he was going to make some changes. He was going to stop his sinful activities and begin to attend church regularly. God did move on the behalf of Jerry and he was able to overcome the illness. However, he only attended church a couple of times and his life went back to business as usual. Sometimes when we are faced with a crisis we make promises to God that we will be different if He brings us through this hardship. However, we need to be careful when we promise God something as the Scripture reads in Eccelesiastes 5:4-7:

4 When you make a vow to God, do not delay to fulfill it. He has no pleasure in fools; fulfill your vow.

5 It is better not to make a vow than to make one and not fulfill it.

6 Do not let your mouth lead you into sin. And do not protest to the temple messenger, "My vow was a mistake." Why should God be angry at what you say and destroy the work of your hands?

7 Much dreaming and many words are meaningless. Therefore fear God.

My friend Jerry and Pharoah both made the same mistake. When they were faced with a crisis they made a vow to God that they would do something in return if He would relieve the suffering. God did relieve the suffering but then the vow was not kept. I am not sure how Jerry's story will end, hopefully on a good note, but we do know from Scripture what happened to Pharoah.

God next sends a plague of darkness upon Pharoah. This would seem to exemplify the darkness of Pharoah's heart and of the Egyptian people in general. This time Pharoah summoned Moses and told him that all the people could go to worship including the women and children but just not the livestock. This posed another problem as they needed livestock to sacrifice. However, Pharoah again refused to let them go. This time Pharoah gave Moses the warning that if he ever appeared before him again that Pharoah would see to his death. Moses states that he will indeed never appear before Pharoah again. The situation had gotten to a drastic point and God was going to send one more plague that would convince Pharoah to allow the people of Israel to leave. In fact, he would desire them to go and the Egyptian people would give them gifts as they left.

The final plague was that every firstborn in Egypt would die. This plague would be somewhat different in that it seemed that it could have an impact on the Israelites as well. God had made a remedy for that. Each Israelite household needed to take a year-old sheep or goat and sacrifice it. They then would put the blood on the doorposts of each home and they would not be impacted by the plague of the firstborn male dying. A wonderful Scripture is found in Exodus 12:13: "The blood will be a sign for you on the houses where you are, and when I see the blood, I will pass over you. No destructive plague will touch you when I strike Egypt." This is a beautiful Scripture because it foreshadows what Christ has done for us. Jesus came to earth as God and man at the same time. He lived a perfect life and died as a sacrifice for the sins of others. Therefore, whoever will repent of their sin and trust in Christ can have forgiveness and eternal life. The sacrifice of a lamb and putting the blood on the doorpost is a wonderful picture of how the blood of Christ will protect every Christian from God's wrath.

The effects of this last plague were devastating for the Egyptians as every household had someone dead. Exodus 12:30 tells us: "Pharoah and his officials and all the Egyptians got up during the night, and there was loud wailing in Egypt, for there was not a house without someone dead." What a truly horrible night for the Egyptian people.

Pharoah was deeply impacted by the deaths as he summoned Moses and Aaron during the night and told them to leave and take everything with them. He also says something very curious at this time. He asks Moses and Aaron to bless him. This seems like a strange request for Pharoah to make unless he was having change of heart. At this point in the narrative one may begin to believe that perhaps Pharoah had finally experienced true repentance.

However, the repentance was not genuine. Pharoah had not changed his mind or actions towards the Israelites. It should be remembered that for repentance to be genuine there needs to a change in mind and action. Pharoah would exhibit neither. Exodus 14:5-6 reads: "When the king of Egypt was told that the people had fled, Pharoah and his officials changed their minds about them and said, 'What have we done? We have let the Israelites go and have lost their services! 'So he had his chariot made ready and took his army with him." It is interesting that the Scripture even states that Pharoah and the officials changed their minds. Changing our minds about sin is the essence of repentance. It seems that Pharoah had made an emotional decision to repent of the sin of disobeying God. However, when the emotions began to subside and it seemed that the hardship had passed he revealed that his repentance was not real. He returned to his old ways of disobeying God. We must be sure that this is never the story of our lives in that we only have a false repentance when there is a hardship.

This time the penalty for not repenting would also be severe. The Lord allowed the waters of the Red Sea to part so that the Israelites could cross on dry ground. However, the fate of the Egyptians was much different when they tried to cross. The Scriptures state in Exodus 14:26-28:

<u>26</u> Then the LORD said to Moses, "Stretch out your hand over the sea so that the waters may flow back over the Egyptians and their chariots and horsemen."

<u>27</u> Moses stretched out his hand over the sea, and at daybreak the sea went back to its place. The Egyptians were fleeing toward it, and the LORD swept them into the sea.

<u>28</u> The water flowed back and covered the chariots and horsemen—the entire army of Pharaoh that had followed the Israelites into the sea. Not one of them survived.

This would be a severe penalty for Egypt which would have left them crippled. Not only had there been those that died in the households but now the army, along with many of the military and political leaders, were dead not to mention the equipment lost. This type of loss would take a long time to recover from as well as leave them vulnerable to surrounding nations.

The penalty of Pharoah's refusal to repent was indeed severe. As well, the penalty for each one that does not repent of their sin and trust in Christ will be severe. The penalty for our sin is an eternity in a place called hell being totally separated from ever experiencing God's presence, love or blessings. However, the good news is that God does not desire this for anyone. He has made a way through trusting in Christ that we can avoid this penalty for our sin. Pharoah never did repent and turn to the one true God and it cost him everything. My hope is that no one reading this book will make the same error.

REPENTANCE WITH DAVID AND SAUL

In considering repentance let's now look at two men who lived several centuries after Moses and Pharoah. Those two men are David and Saul and they lived in the same time period with one another and had multiple interactions with one another. They had similar backgrounds in that they both had their time as the king of Israel. They also had the similarity that they both made huge mistakes while they were the king. The great difference between them was how they reacted after they had committed the sin. That is also the key in our lives. We have all sinned but the important point is how we react to our sin. We may be sorry for our sin but not actually repent and that is not pleasing to God. However, God is pleased when we admit our sin and repent meaning that if we could go back in time we would change what happened. That is the major difference between Saul and David. David seemed to desire to change his past sins while this is not seen in Saul.

Let's look at the life of Saul first. Saul was called to be king from the tribe of Benjamin. He was a tall and stately looking man, the type that looked like he should be the leader of a people. One day Saul's father, Kish, asked his son to take a servant and go looking for the flocks. After a time they could not find the flocks in the wilderness and so Saul desired to go back so that his father would not worry about him. However, Saul's servant suggested that they go and ask the man of God who was in a nearby village. The man of God that was suggested was one of God's great prophets, Samuel. God had already spoken to Samuel the day before and told him that Saul would be coming as I Samuel 9:15-16 tells us: "Now the day before Saul came, the Lord had revealed this to Samuel: 'About this time tomorrow I will send you a man from the land of Bemjamin. Anoint him ruler over my people Israel; he will deliver them from the hand of the Philistines. I have looked on my people, for their cry has reached me.'" It seemed like a random meeting to Saul and his servant in which they would just be getting information. However, nothing is random with God as he often uses seemingly chance circumstances to change the course of a life.

Samuel tells Saul that he will become the leader of Israel. In the beginning Saul is a seemingly humble man who does not embrace the idea of leadership as he says in I Samuel 9:21: "Saul answered, 'But am I not a Benjaminite, from the smallest tribe of Israel, and is not my clan the least of all the clans of the tribe of Benjamin? Why do you say such a thing to me?'" This beginning speech of humility is something that is heard several times when God calls leaders. It is later that they become corrupted with the idea of the power they have come to obtain and go down a wrong path. Many a leader in various areas of life has begun with good intentions only to later become corrupted when they do not hold firm to biblical principles.

Samuel proceeds to tell Saul what will occur in his life over the next couple of days. This culminates with I Samuel 10:5-7 and the words that Samuel is prophesying to Saul: "'After that you will go to Gibeah of God, where there is a Philistine outpost. As you approach the town, you will meet a procession of prophets coming down from the high place with lyres, timbrels, pipes and harps being played before them, and they will be prophesying. The Spirit of the Lord will come powerfully upon you, and you will prophesy with them; and you will be changed into a different person. Once these signs are fulfilled, do whatever your hand finds to do, for God is with you.'" It is important to note the strong beginning that Saul had before we lament his sad ending. Often, we can start in the right direction but Satan is doing all that he can to bring each person to a point of sin and denial of God. Unfortunately, this is the path that the life of Saul would take.

After being anointed and prophesying Saul went back to a somewhat normal life and did not tell those closest to him all that had happened. A little while later there was a time when Samuel was going to anoint a king. It is of interest to note that this was not what God desired. He wanted the people of Israel to have God as their king but they continued asking for a king and God granted their wish although it would ultimately be to their detriment. When the time came for Saul to be anointed king he hid among the supplies. Perhaps this is a glimpse of the true character of Saul as he was reluctant to take his place as Israel's leader although God had told Samuel to anoint him and he had experienced being among the prophets. In spite of these events Saul was still hiding from his calling.

Saul once again went back to his normal life after the announcement but shortly thereafter there was a disturbance in Israel and Saul felt led to intervene. I Samuel 11:6 tells us: "When Saul heard these words, the Spirit of God came powerfully upon him, and he burned with anger." God used Saul to deliver Israel from their enemy and, after that, the people desired to install Saul as king. Saul even reveals that he is still on the right track to a certain level at this time as he refuses to put to death those Israelites who did not initially believe he should be their leader.

It was not too long after Saul became king that there began to be problems with his obedience. There was a situation in which Israel was in battle against their enemies and Saul was their military leader as well as king. It was important that Samuel come and offer a burnt offering for them to be victorious. However, the appointed time for Samuel to arrive had come and gone. The troops were now quaking with fear and Saul felt compelled to take matters into his own hands without waiting for God's timing and ways. Saul decided to offer the burnt offering himself even though he knew this was forbidden. It must have an awkward moment when Samuel arrived just as Saul had finished the offering. The next few moments were critical for Saul's future and this is what transpired in I Samuel 13:

> <u>11</u> "What have you done?" asked Samuel. Saul replied, "When I saw that the men were scattering, and that you did not come at the set time, and that the Philistines were assembling at Mikmash,
>
> <u>12</u> I thought, 'Now the Philistines will come down against me at Gilgal, and I have not sought the LORD's favor.' So I felt compelled to offer the burnt offering."

13 "You have done a foolish thing," Samuel said. "You have not kept the command the LORD your God gave you; if you had, he would have established your kingdom over Israel for all time.

14 But now your kingdom will not endure; the LORD has sought out a man after his own heart and appointed him ruler of his people, because you have not kept the LORD's command."

This was the beginning of the end for Saul. A key factor here is that when Saul was somewhat caught in the act of doing something against God's plan that his initial reaction was not to repent but to offer a reason for his rebellion. Perhaps if Saul had been willing to admit his sin and repent everything could have been different. All sin is able to be forgiven when there is repentance. I know that many people might think that offering a sacrifice on his own does not seem nearly as bad as other sins that were committed by major Bible characters. However, the difference is not the severity of the sin but the attitude of the heart after the sin has been revealed. This is still true today. Many people have committed what we think of as severe sins and been forgiven because they truly repented. However, others have lived a fairly clean life but never find forgiveness because they are not truly sorry and refuse to repent.

I have not always been the best at admitting my sin but an instance where God did lead me in the right direction and I followed comes to mind. There was a friend and I who had been engaging in activities that we knew were a sin. One day they came to visit and they wanted to discuss it. They had the attitude of what was really wrong with what we were doing as no one was being harmed. I responded that we should not go down that road. What we were doing was a sin and to try and pretend that it is not was going down a dangerous path. God used this conversation to further convict me of the sin which ultimately led to true repentance. I lost touch with the friend so I am not sure what decision they made in the end. I am thankful that God led me to recognize the sin and repent before there were worse consequences. It seems that this is something that did not happen for Saul as he seemed to be unwilling to admit his sin in this area.

Another aspect that needs to be discussed is the idea that some may think that the pronouncement of God's judgment was announced rather quickly for Saul. However, on this front we must remember that God knows every heart and the decisions that they will make in the end. God knew Saul's heart and that he ultimately would be unwilling to repent of this action no matter how long he was given. We must remember that God gives us an opportunity to repent and ask for forgiveness through Christ and that God is not obligated to offer us the chance to repent and seek forgiveness multiple times. The Bible tells us in II Corinthians 6:1-2: "As God's co-workers we urge you not to receive God's grace in vain. For he says, 'In the time of my favor I heard you, and in the day of salvation I helped you.' I tell you, now is the time of God's favor, now is the day of salvation." It is interesting to note that this was written to believers as they are even called 'co-workers.' When we hear God's conviction of sin and call to repentance, whether Christian or non-Christian, it behooves us to make an immediate response.

However, much to his detriment, making an immediate move to repentance was something that Saul did not do. Saul had this act of disobedience that he had not repented of weighing in his life when another opportunity to follow the instructions of the Lord occurred. God was about to punish the Amalekites who were a strong enemy of Israel. Saul was presented with specific instructions when he receives this message through Samuel in I Samuel 15:3: "Now go, attack the Amalekites and totally destroy all that belongs to them. Do not spare them, put to death men and women, children and infants, cattle and sheep, camels and donkeys." The instructions were clear. At times God's instructions to us are crystal clear and we must decide how to respond.

The Lord gave Saul and the Israelites a great victory. However, we see his response in I Samuel 15:8-9: "He took Agag king of the Amalekites alive, and all his people he totally destroyed with the sword. But Saul and the army spared Agag and the best of the sheep and cattle, the fat calves and lambs-everything that was good. These they were unwilling to destroy completely, but everything that was despised and weak they totally destroyed." One must wonder what got into Saul to think that he could disobey God's clear command. Sometimes we must ask what gets into us when we similarly disobey God's clear command.

The Lord even said in verse 11 that He regretted that he had made Saul king. Saul's actions also angered Samuel and he cried out all night to God. However, the situation got even worse as I Samuel 15:12 states: "Early in the morning Samuel got up and went to meet Saul, but he was told, 'Saul has gone to Carmel. There he has set up a monument in his own honor and has turned and gone on down to Gilgal.'" Saul seems to be so blind to his lack of obedience and repentance that he thinks he deserves honor. He is even willing to set up a monument in his own honor. We must remember that the Bible tells us in Proverbs that pride goes before a fall and be wary whenever we find ourselves wanting to set up opportunities to bring honor to ourselves.

In light of this, what follows must have been an embarrassing situation. Saul is thinking that he is worthy of honor but something else is about to happen. The Bible tells us I Samuel 15:13-21:

13 When Samuel reached him, Saul said, "The LORD bless you! I have carried out the LORD's instructions."

14 But Samuel said, "What then is this bleating of sheep in my ears? What is this lowing of cattle that I hear?"

15 Saul answered, "The soldiers brought them from the Amalekites; they spared the best of the sheep and cattle to sacrifice to the LORD your God, but we totally destroyed the rest."

16 "Enough!" Samuel said to Saul. "Let me tell you what the LORD said to me last night." "Tell me," Saul replied.

17 Samuel said, "Although you were once small in your own eyes, did you not become the head of the tribes of Israel? The LORD anointed you king over Israel.

18 And he sent you on a mission, saying, 'Go and completely destroy those wicked people, the Amalekites; wage war against them until you have wiped them out.'

19 Why did you not obey the LORD? Why did you pounce on the plunder and do evil in the eyes of the LORD?"

20 "But I did obey the LORD," Saul said. "I went on the mission the LORD assigned me. I completely destroyed the Amalekites and brought back Agag their king.

21 The soldiers took sheep and cattle from the plunder, the best of what was devoted to God, in order to sacrifice them to the LORD your God at Gilgal."

To begin with, Saul flat out lies to Samuel and tells him that they have obeyed the Lord's instructions. It is interesting that Saul would choose to lie to Sameul. Perhaps Saul had temporarily forgotten that Samuel was God's prophet and as such he often had God's provision in discerning the truth. Samuel responds by telling him that he can hear the sheep and the cattle that were not slaughtered. If we could look back in time we might see Saul's face turning red with embarrassment at this time. Or perhaps Saul was already beyond this type of reaction.

This is another critical juncture in Saul's life. Perhaps if Saul had understood and admitted his sin then things would have been different. However, instead of repenting of his disobedience to the Lord, Saul tries to make excuses for his sin. Whenever we go down the path of excuses rather than repentance we are headed towards trouble. Saul refuses to admit that his lack of complete obedience is actually disobedience. Saul thought that because he was going to sacrifice the animals that he took then it was fine to disobey God's command. However, it is more difficult to explain why he preserved the life of the Agag the Amalekite king.

God then gives a message to Saul that still rings true today. I Samuel 15:22 states the Lord's words: "But Samuel replied: 'Does the Lord delight in burnt offerings and sacrifices as much as in obeying the Lord? To obey is better than sacrifice, and to heed is better than the fat of rams.'" God makes it clear for all time that the most important aspect to Him is complete obedience. This is true even when we are supposedly making a great sacrifice and hoping that the Lord will disregard our disobedience.

After this pronouncement Saul seems to be moved towards admitting his sin as he states in I Samuel 15:24-25: "The Saul said to Samuel, 'I have sinned. I violated the Lord's command and your instructions. I was afraid of the men and so I gave in to them. Now I beg you, forgive my sin and come back with me, so that I may worship the Lord.'" Two aspects of Saul's confession would seem to make it unacceptable to the Lord. The first is that he fails to take full responsibility for his sin. Rather he states the men were the ones who led him to this disobedience. This rings similar to Adam and Eve as they both blamed something else rather than taking responsibility for their actions. God is most pleased when we admit that we have sinned, seek forgiveness for the sin that is our own fault and desire to turn away from that sin. A second reason that Saul's confession would seem to be unpleasing to the Lord is that he likely has the ulterior motive of wanting to get back to worshipping God, most presumably because it would help him in his war mission and so that he would look good in front of the people. Saul reveals this motive in I Samuel 15:30: "Saul replied, 'I have sinned. But please honor me before the elders of my people and before Israel, come back with me, so that I may worship the Lord your God.'" Saul does not seem to understand the gravity of his sin and thinks that if he just admits it then everything can be restored. However, it seems that deep in his heart that Saul is not truly wanting to change his ways and experience true repentance. Whenever we simply admit our sin because we are caught without truly desiring to change and have a different outcome the next time then our actions do not please God.

The Bible tells us that, unfortunately for Saul, this was the last time Samuel and Saul would see one another this side of the grave. As well, we are told that Samuel mourned for Saul. I suppose it was difficult for Samuel to see Saul go down the path of disobedience without repentance. When a person turns their back on the path of following God there are often unexpected consequences and unexpected people that are harmed.

Of course, everything could have been different for Saul. He made mistakes and sinned but the key to Saul's life is that he would not repent of the evil and disobedience that he had done. In fact, looking good in front of others even became more important to him than having a right standing and relationship with God. Another critical point for Saul is that he did not see the importance of his sin. We need to see the importance of all sin in the eyes of God. There is no rebellion against God and His commands that He see as minor. He calls us to repent and seek forgiveness of all sin. Saul was about to be replaced by David. A man who would also make mistakes and sin but whose attitude towards repentance would be very different.

DAVID

The beginnings of David and Saul's call to service had some similarity. Both of them were unlikely in the thoughts of people to be called to be a king but for different reasons. As we learned earlier, Saul came from an obscure tribe and family that normally would not produce a king. However, David had several older brothers that would seem to be better leadership material. Saul looked like a man that people would expect to be a leader while the Bible describes David as young and not even thought by his father, Jesse, to be someone who would be considered for leadership. The calling of David is worth looking at for the lesson it teaches us. I Samuel 16:6-12 reads:

> <u>6</u> When they arrived, Samuel saw Eliab and thought, "Surely the LORD's anointed stands here before the LORD."

7 But the LORD said to Samuel, "Do not consider his appearance or his height, for I have rejected him. The LORD does not look at the things people look at. People look at the outward appearance, but the LORD looks at the heart."

8 Then Jesse called Abinadab and had him pass in front of Samuel. But Samuel said, "The LORD has not chosen this one either."

9 Jesse then had Shammah pass by, but Samuel said, "Nor has the LORD chosen this one."

10 Jesse had seven of his sons pass before Samuel, but Samuel said to him, "The LORD has not chosen these."

11 So he asked Jesse, "Are these all the sons you have?" "There is still the youngest," Jesse answered. "He is tending the sheep." Samuel said, "Send for him; we will not sit down until he arrives."

12 So he sent for him and had him brought in. He was glowing with health and had a fine appearance and handsome features. Then the LORD said, "Rise and anoint him; this is the one."

Notice how even a wise and godly man like Samuel was fooled by the physical appearance of the first son. He thought he would be anointed king because he looked like he fit the part. We do not base decisions as much on appearance today as they did then. However, our problem in this area is that we tend to look at an individual's credentials in deciding if they will be a good leader. Looking only at credentials may work better in the world but in the church we should be more concerned with a person's godly character rather than their resume. As well, we often think that because someone is good at something in a secular profession then it logically follows that they will also be good in that type of work in the church. However, God grants Christians spiritual gifts that do not necessarily coincide with being proficient in a secular profession.

I remember a humorous conversation with a friend a few years back about whether or not a pastor would make a good manager in a secular business. We decided that pastors are given a gift to be used in the church but this does not necessarily mean that they would be proficient in a secular management position. If we all know this is true then we should not expect that the person that is proficient at a secular position would be able to do the same when working in God's kingdom. Working in God's kingdom depends on spiritual gifting.

Thus, David was unexpectedly anointed as king. I am sure that was a surprise to not only Samuel but also to Jesse and his seven other sons. As we all know, David has several victories early in his life such as defeating Goliath and still honoring Saul as God's called king even though Saul was trying to kill him. These are some of the most famous stories in the Bible and worthy of following David as an example in these instances. However, for our purposes we are not as concerned with when David behaved heroically but how he responded to his sin.

By this time in his life David has become the king, just as Samuel said, and has won many battles for Israel. It was the spring of the year and kings often went off to fight their enemies at that time of year. However, for some reason David sent the army out with a trusted man and chose to stay home. It was here that the trouble would come into play. That evening David went up on the roof and saw a beautiful woman bathing. Of course, David should have turned away immediately. Most likely, if he had been in a close relationship with the Lord at that time in his life he would not have given a second glance.

However, David did not turn away and instead made the decision to allow lust to build in his heart. Whenever we are tempted it is best to turn away immediately. The Bible even tells us to flee from the temptations that Satan puts before us in James 4:7: "Submit yourselves, then, to God. Resist the devil, and he will flee from you." Jesus also has especially strong words about the type of temptation David experienced as He tells us in Matthew 5:28: "But I tell you that anyone who looks at a woman lustfully has already committed adultery with her in his heart." These words may seem shocking to hear with the direction our culture is going but God's standards are still true today. Jesus said a person commits the sin of adultery in his heart when they look at someone lustfully and that standard has not changed.

Thus, we can see that when David pauses to take a longer glance at Bathsheba he has already committed adultery in his heart. If he had stopped there he could have avoided a lot of heartache but he did not. David now made his second error by sending someone to ask about her. The messenger tells him that she is Uriah's wife. If David were acting honorably at this time he would have especially refused to sleep with the wife of a man that was fighting battles for the nation of which he is king. When we allow temptation to linger and begin to take action on our initial thought then we are moving away from God's path for us. David was further entangled when he sent messengers to get her. David then allows his temptation to come to fruition as he sleeps with Bathsheba. It seems amazing that this all happens in just one evening. David must have allowed his heart to drift away from the Lord and he was ripe for temptation.

David soon receives devastating news as Bathsheba sends a message to him saying that she is now pregnant with his child. David is not willing to give up his integrity that easily as he sends for Uriah to come home. David does not realize that he may be preserving an outward show of integrity but he has already lost it in God's eyes. When Uriah arrives from the battle David uses the occasion to ask about the other military men and how the battle is going. David then encourages Uriah to go and stay at his home, of course, hoping that Uriah would sleep with his wife and that he would believe the child was his. However, Uriah does something shocking. He refuses to go to spend the night in his own home when the other soldiers are staying in tents. Uriah says it this way in II Samuel 11:11: "Uriah said to David, 'The ark and Israel and Judah are staying in tents, and my commander Joab and my lord's men are camped in the open country. How could I go to my house to eat and drink and make love to my wife? As surely as you live, I will not do such a thing." David is frustrated by this and requests for Uriah to stay one more day. On that second night David invited Uriah to eat and drink with him. The results were that Uriah became drunk. Surely, he would go be with his wife when he was drunk but he did not. He rather chose once again to sleep at the entrance to the palace with the other servants.

It is interesting to note the stark difference between David and Uriah as this point. David is described as a man after God's own heart and acted honorably when he chose not to harm Saul because he was God's anointed king even though Saul was trying to kill him. Now David is definitely not acting with honor. Uriah is the one in this instance that is acting in a way that pleased God. As well, David had all of the spiritual advantages over Uriah as he had seen God work in miraculous ways in his life but is less honorable that Uriah. Now David is choosing a different path and it will cost him dearly.

The next action that David decides on is even more heinous than before. David sends Uriah back with a note for the commanding officer. II Samuel 11:15 reads: "In it he wrote, 'Put Uriah out in front where the fighting is fiercest. Then withdraw from him so will be struck down and die." It is truly amazing that David would shrink to such a level after being at such heights earlier in his life. It helps us to understand that every person is capable of despicable acts. It is only God's grace that keeps each person from exhibiting similar behavior.

The events in the battle occur just as David planned and Uriah is killed. The Scripture tells what happens next and, predictably, how the Lord views it in II Samuel 11:26-27: "When Uriah's wife heard that her husband was dead, she mourned for him. After the time of mourning was over, David had her brought to his house, and she became his wife and bore him a son. But the thing displeased the Lord." David had been such a tremendous servant of the Lord and now the Scripture says that the Lord is displeased with these events in his life.

Of course, David was a servant of the true and living God and He was not going to allow this sinful act to go without notice. We must always remember that if we are truly a born again part of the family of

God then He will send discipline for our disobedience. When God sends discipline on one of His children the goal is for them to repent and remember the horror of their sin so that they can possibly resist it the next time.

God was going to send someone to call David to account for his sin. That someone was the prophet Nathan. We are not told exactly how long it is after the death of Uriah that God sends Nathan but it is apparently most likely between nine months and a year as the child of David and Bathsheba was already born but from the text he still seems to be just a few months old.

The prophet Nathan came to David and shared a fictional story with him about two men that lived in a certain town. One man was rich and the other poor. The poor man had only one lamb that he loved dearly. When a traveler came to town the rich man did not take one of his many sheep to feed him but rather took the only lamb of the poor man. When the story was finished David reacted by saying that the rich man should be killed and forced to pay four times what he had taken from the poor man. Of course, David did not realize that the story was really about him. The outrage and pronouncement that he made against the rich man was going to be used by God in crafting David's penalty for his sin as Nathan responded with these words in II Samuel 12:7-12.

> 7 Then Nathan said to David, "You are the man! This is what the LORD, the God of Israel, says: 'I anointed you king over Israel, and I delivered you from the hand of Saul.
>
> 8 I gave your master's house to you, and your master's wives into your arms. I gave you all Israel and Judah. And if all this had been too little, I would have given you even more.
>
> 9 Why did you despise the word of the LORD by doing what is evil in his eyes? You struck down Uriah the Hittite with the sword and took his wife to be your own. You killed him with the sword of the Ammonites.

10 Now, therefore, the sword will never depart from your house, because you despised me and took the wife of Uriah the Hittite to be your own.'

11 "This is what the LORD says: 'Out of your own household I am going to bring calamity on you. Before your very eyes I will take your wives and give them to one who is close to you, and he will sleep with your wives in broad daylight.

12 You did it in secret, but I will do this thing in broad daylight before all Israel.' "

David had now been confronted with his sin. His next move in his relationship with the Lord was critical. Whenever we realize that we have sinned against the Lord how we respond is crucial. David responded to Nathan's words by simply saying that he had sinned against the Lord. The Lord replied through Nathan that David's sin had been forgiven but as an earthly penalty for this sin the child born to he and Bathsheba would die. David prayed, fasted and pleaded with God that the child would not die but in the end the child did die. After the child had died

David then went into the house of the Lord and worshiped.

Of course, the sin that David committed was horrible but what he did when confronted with his sin is a model for how our response should be. First of all, David admitted his sin. He did not blame anyone else or make excuses. He knew that what he had done was a sin and admitted it. David could not go back and take away the death of Uriah but he revealed his repentant heart by going to the house of the Lord to worship. This repentance is the second key to how David responded to his sin. If we look at David's life after these events and how the Lord worked through him to write Scripture and lead the people we can see that David had truly repented of his sin. The two keys from looking at David's sin are to admit our sin and repent, or turn away from it.

We can see how David felt about his sin in Psalm 51 which was written after his sin with Bathsheba and the murder of Uriah. In Psalm 51:1-4 David is a tremendous example of taking responsibility for sin and not blaming others:

> 1 Have mercy on me, O God, according to your unfailing love; according to your great compassion blot out my transgressions.
>
> 2 Wash away all my iniquity and cleanse me from my sin.
>
> 3 For I know my transgressions, and my sin is always before me.
>
> 4 Against you, you only, have I sinned and done what is evil in your sight; so you are right in your verdict and justified when you judge.

David takes responsibility for his sin and states that he knows that God was justified in his judgment. A few verses later David calls upon the Lord to help him to have a clean heart revealing that he understands the magnitude of his sin and how it displeases the Lord as he wrote in verses 10 and 11: "Create in me a pure heart, O God, and renew a steadfast spirit within me. Do not cast me from your presence or take your Holy Spirit from me." It is interesting that David requests a pure heart and a renewed steadfast spirit. It seems that David is looking back at the majority of his life and how that he was steady in his devotion to God and longs to get back to that point. Perhaps you can look back at your life and see a point when your walk with God was more steady. We can always return to that. God desires that for our lives also and he is waiting for us to return to a reliable walk with Him. I remember a time in my life when I had allowed myself to drift from a close walk with the Lord. He sent circumstances into my life that allowed me to get back where I needed to be. If you are thinking about a time when your walk with God was more steadfast, He is waiting for your return and wants it even more that you do.

Later in this Psalm David also speaks of his desire to help others to also turn back from their sin as verse 13 intimates: "Then I will teach transgressors your ways, so that sinners will turn back to you." Thus, it can be seen through this Psalm that David takes responsibility for his sin, understands how that he has offended a holy God, desires to change so that he will not commit similar sins and even wants to help other sinners to turn from their disobedience. These are all signs that David has truly repented.

THE DIFFERENCE BETWEEN SAUL AND DAVID

We have looked in some detail at Saul and David and the times in their lives of the greatest failings. There are several differences in how they responded to their sin that are noteworthy. First is the idea of admitting their sin. Saul did not seem to want to admit that he had truly done anything wrong. David admitted that he had sinned. Secondly, when Saul did admit that he had not obeyed God's commands he blamed others. David did not blame others but realized that he was responsible for his own actions. Thirdly, Saul did not seem to recognize the seriousness of his sin. Saul had went against God's wishes by offering sacrifices himself. God intended for this to be done by those He specifically had chosen but Saul did not take this mandate seriously. However, David did take his sin seriously and knew that he had offended a holy God. Finally, Saul did not indicate signs of true repentance. One of the hallmark signs of true repentance is desiring to go back and change the time that the sin was committed but Saul did not reveal that he would have changed his past sinful actions. However, as we can see from David's later life it did appear that he regretted his sins of adultery and murder and wished that he could go back in time and change it.

Another factor to consider is that there were earthly consequences for both Saul and David. Saul lost his kingdom and suffered other difficulties in his life because of his sin. David also suffered for sin with the death of his child and family turmoil. However, the difference is in the how this impacted their relationship with God. David experienced a restored and loving relationship with his Heavenly Father after his repentance. Saul, however, did not experience a closeness to the Lord because he never truly repented.

This reminds us that the worldly penalty for our sins often remains after repentance but our eternal penalties are taken away by the blood of Christ. I have been blessed to have done prison ministry for several years. During that time I had close relationships with several inmates that truly repented of their sin and experienced a wonderful relationship with God and the promise of eternal life. One example I can think of is a man we will call Chad. Chad had been a decent and hard-working man but then allowed anger in one situation to take over his life to the point that he killed another man. He received a life sentence for his crime. After entering prison he trusted Christ and repented of his sin. Chad experiences God's love and presence with him each day in prison but is still serving a life sentence as an earthly consequence for his sin. This is true of many of the inmates that I fellowshipped with. They had repented of their sin and become Christians but their earthly circumstances remained. They were still incarcerated in a prison even after repenting of their sin. God can and does take away the earthly consequences of our sin at times but this is not what happens for the majority of people. Most Christians still live with the earthly consequences of their sin even though they have forgiveness and eternal life. Another example would be of someone who destroyed their health through alcoholism or drug addiction. Later in life they may repent of their actions and receive forgiveness but the impacts on their bodies still remains. God can miraculously heal in these circumstances but that is not the norm. Most of the time people still face the impact on their bodies of their previous sinful lifestyles although they now have eternal forgiveness. It is entirely possible to experience the love and presence of God in our lives while still living with the earthly consequences of our sin.

Some may say that David's sins of adultery and murder were much more serious than Saul's sin and that he should have been forgiven before David was. However, the seriousness of our sin is not the real issue but rather how we respond to our sin. The wages or penalty of our sins, no matter how little or how great, is eternal separation from God. The only way to have our sins forgiven is to repent and trust that Christ was the payment for our sins. Often times people think, perhaps like the sins of Saul, that they are not that bad. However, the Bible tells us in Isaiah 64:6: "All of us have become like one who is unclean, and all our righteousness is like filthy rags, we all shrivel up like a leaf, and like the wind our sins sweep us away." Think about what God is telling us here. All of the good things in our lives that we tend to be so proud of are like filthy rags compared to His perfect righteousness. There is no hope for any of us apart from repenting of our sins and trusting in Christ for forgiveness. Thus, when we look at Saul and David we may think that Saul's sins were not all that bad but to God they were. Again, the key is not how bad our sins appear to people but whether or not there is true repentance. David, although many think his sins were worse, exhibited that true repentance and received forgiveness.

THE OLD TESTAMENT PROPHETS

The prophets in the Old Testament lived in a time when Israel was engaging in a sinful pattern and desperately needed to repent. They continuously preached this message of repentance for hundreds of years. One of the major sins that Israel was committing during this time period was worshipping idols and the prophets called them to repent and begin to worship the one true God.

Although there were instances of renewal during this time, ultimately the majority of the Israelites would not repent and return to God. What resulted was being taken over by the Babylonian empire and most of the Israelites being taken into captivity for 70 years. Of course, this could have been avoided if the people would have repented and turned back to God. This is a beneficial lesson for us today. God gives people ample opportunity to repent but in the end the judgement that He foretells will come to pass if they do not turn away from their sin.

Let's take some time to explore some of the relevant passages from the Old Testament prophet's call to repentance that are recorded in Scripture. Ezekiel 14:1-6 tells us:

<u>1</u> Some of the elders of Israel came to me and sat down in front of me.

<u>2</u> Then the word of the LORD came to me:

<u>3</u> "Son of man, these men have set up idols in their hearts and put wicked stumbling blocks before their faces. Should I let them inquire of me at all?

<u>4</u> Therefore speak to them and tell them, 'This is what the Sovereign LORD says: When any of the Israelites set up idols in their hearts and put a wicked stumbling block before their faces and then go to a prophet, I the LORD will answer them myself in keeping with their great idolatry.

<u>5</u> I will do this to recapture the hearts of the people of Israel, who have all deserted me for their idols.'

<u>6</u> "Therefore say to the people of Israel, 'This is what the Sovereign LORD says: Repent! Turn from your idols and renounce all your detestable practices!

The prophetic ministry of Ezekiel was ended with the exile to Babylon. He is giving this prophecy after years of God calling the people to repent. Their rebellion would soon result in a harsh judgment although they seem to not believe that it actually would happen. The elders most likely recognized the ministry of Ezekiel in some capacity as they came and sat down in front of him to hear what response he would give to their inquiry.

The Word of the Lord came to Ezekiel telling him the state of the elders' hearts. The Lord informs Ezekiel that they have set up idols in their hearts and allowed a stumbling block into their lives. The Lord speaks to Ezekiel about the idea that they should not be allowed to bring inquiry to the Lord due to the state of their hearts. This is a very serious thing to consider for us. It appears that the Lord would not hear their inquiry because they had not repented of their sin. Perhaps many prayers go unanswered today because people have not repented of their sin.

The Lord then tells Ezekiel that when an Israelite has sin in their heart and does not repent that God Himself will answer their question or prayer. God states that He will do this in order to recapture their hearts. This reveals how great God's love is for His people. Although they have strayed from the Lord for generations He still calls for them to repent and have a restored relationship. However, for the people of Israel there came a time when judgment would come and there was no more time to repent. God is a loving and merciful God but there is a time in the life of each person that refuses to repent when God will close that door and bring judgment. We must remember that this is not God's desire or plan but it is a result of sin that has not been repented of.

In verse 6 we read what God's ultimate message to them is as He calls them to repent. For the elders of Israel that day of repenting meant for them to turn from their idols and their detestable practices. Of course, the elders, along with the majority of the nation, would not repent. Ultimately, God's judgment came upon them.

God calls each person today to repent. Although the details of repentance may look different for each individual the results of a restored relationship with our Heavenly Father are the same. For those who refuse to repent judgment will ultimately come.

Another prophet from this time period was Isaiah and he lived roughly 100 years before Ezekiel and yet he had a similar message of repentance. This reveals how longsuffering God is. He was calling Israel to repentance for well over 100 years before bringing judgment. Isaiah 45:17-22 reads:

17 But Israel will be saved by the LORD with an everlasting salvation; you will never be put to shame or disgraced, to ages everlasting.

18 For this is what the LORD says— he who created the heavens, he is God; he who fashioned and made the earth, he founded it; he did not create it to be empty, but formed it to be inhabited— he says: "I am the LORD, and there is no other.

19 I have not spoken in secret, from somewhere in a land of darkness; I have not said to Jacob's descendants, 'Seek me in vain.' I, the LORD, speak the truth; I declare what is right.

20 "Gather together and come; assemble, you fugitives from the nations. Ignorant are those who carry about idols of wood, who pray to gods that cannot save.

21 Declare what is to be, present it— let them take counsel together. Who foretold this long ago, who declared it from the distant past? Was it not I, the LORD? And there is no God apart from me, a righteous God and a Savior; there is none but me.

22 "Turn to me and be saved, all you ends of the earth; for I am God, and there is no other."

In verse 17 God is predicting that Israel will eventually be saved. However, in the following verses He states that a change must be made for this to be a reality. God reminds the listeners that He is the creator of all the earth in verse 18. Since He is the creator of all then it logically follows that His rules should apply when it comes to salvation. Often, people begin to believe that they can make up their own rules about salvation. The Israelites thought that way 2700 years ago and many people still think that way today. God's rules about salvation still prevail. People, in our natural pride, begin to believe that someone can obtain salvation by all of the good works that they do. However, God clearly tells us that salvation only comes by admitting to our sinful condition and trusting in Christ as our savior.

In verse 19 the Lord reminds them that He has not spoken His truth in secret but that He desires for all the Israelites to know the way of salvation. The same is true today. For all those who truly seek to know God's truth about salvation He will allow them to find the way.

In verses 20 and 21 God speaks about those who worship idols made of wood as a substitute for Him. God reiterates the fact that He is the only God and everything else that the Israelites worship is false. This is also truth for our time. People often put something else above God by making it more important than Him. In modern times, people rarely bow down physically and worship something made of wood or stone. However, we often do something similar in our hearts. Whenever anything takes the place of God in our lives then it has become an idol. The Hebrew word translated 'turn' in verse 22 is penu. It can also be translated as 'look' but has the idea that, whether 'looking' or 'turning,' that a change has been made. God is telling them that in order for them to have salvation that something has to occur first. They need to make a conscious effort to turn to Him. He uses the prophets to tell the people of their need to turn and He makes it easy for them, but in the end they must make the decision to 'turn' to Him which would include the idea of repenting of their idol worship. Today, God calls individuals to salvation through His word and creates every opportunity for them to turn to Him. However, in the end, each person must decide for themselves to turn to God and away from their sin.

This concludes a sampling of Old Testament passages that deal with repentance in the lives of individuals and nations. When we consider the idea of repentance in the Old Testament it was different to a degree because they were looking forward to the Messiah coming. However, the idea of being sorry for sin and desiring to make a change in turning away from sin remains the same. True repentance only happened, as is true today, when there was a desire to turn away from sin. The people living in the Old Testament period were looking forward to a coming Savior who would provide forgiveness. In our times the Savior, Jesus, has come and God asks us to repent of our sin and trust in the sacrifice that Jesus made for our sins.

CHAPTER 4
REPENTANCE IN THE BOOKS OF ACTS AND THE EPISTLES

After looking at the idea of repentance in the Old Testament we will now delve into the teachings about repentance found in the book of Acts and the Epistles. The New Testament has a slightly different outlook because it is after Christ has come. However, the idea of repentance was in the Old Testament as well, as previously studied, although with an idea of looking forwards to the coming of the Messiah. In the New Testament we find the instructions for how believers are to conduct their lives today. We will not cover all of the New Testament passages about repentance but we will look at a few to understand the general flavor of what God presented to us in the New Testament. Much of the passages we look at will seem to say similar things but we want to firmly establish the idea that repentance and trusting in Christ go together in Scripture.

One important aspect to understand about the book of Acts and the Epistles is that they were written to give Christians instructions on doctrinal truth and on how God expects them to live. Thus, for the most part the idea of repentance is presupposed. When God is giving instructions on how to live the Christian life then there is the implied understanding that they would have already repented of their sins and have a desire to live for God. As mentioned before, if someone does not care about how God instructed them to live in the New Testament then this is a good indication that they need to check their own salvation. With this in mind let's look at what the Book of Acts records about repentance.

REPENTANCE IN THE BOOK OF ACTS

In the early chapters of Acts we are allowed a glimpse of an exciting time. The Resurrection of Jesus is still fresh in the minds of the disciples and they are beginning to preach about trusting in Christ for salvation with the result of many people coming to faith. One of the earliest sermons is given by Peter and is recorded in Acts 2. After hearing the stirring message the people asked what they needed to do in Acts 2:37-41:

> **37** When the people heard this, they were cut to the heart and said to Peter and the other apostles, "Brothers, what shall we do?"
>
> **38** Peter replied, "Repent and be baptized, every one of you, in the name of Jesus Christ for the forgiveness of your sins. And you will receive the gift of the Holy Spirit.
>
> **39** The promise is for you and your children and for all who are far off—for all whom the Lord our God will call."
>
> **40** With many other words he warned them; and he pleaded with them, "Save yourselves from this corrupt generation."
>
> **41** Those who accepted his message were baptized, and about three thousand were added to their number that day.

It is worth noting that the first word that Peter replies to the people asking about salvation is to repent. Imagine how excited Peter would have been. He had just preached a powerful message and now the people seem interested and are asking what they need to do. It would have been easy for Peter to give a softer reply. Peter could have told them that all they needed to do was believe and could have not mentioned repentance at all. However, I think that Peter had a Spirit inspired knowledge here as he understood that simply believing without an accompanying desire to turn away from sin is not going to produce the result of a person being born again. When Peter had this opportunity to share with people who were spiritually hungry he wanted to make sure that they understood the need to repent by turning away from sin. Perhaps in our message to the world today it would be beneficial to preach the tandem ideas of believing in Jesus and repentance of sin.

In Acts 3 God uses Peter to heal a lame man who is begging. This miracle draws the attention of the people and soon a crowd has formed around Peter and John. Peter seizes the opportunity to preach to them about Jesus. During his sermon Peter does not hesitate to make sure that the crowd understands the need to repent and believe as he states in verse 19: "Repent, then, and turn to God, so that your sins may be wiped out, that times of refreshing may come from the Lord." Peter makes sure that the interested people understand that it is more than simply believing.

A person must also be willing to turn away from their sin in repentance.

After the truth has been proclaimed in many places, Peter is involved in an incident with a sorcerer named Simon in Acts 8. This Simon became a believer and had seemingly left his sinful life of practicing witchcraft behind. However, after some time he faced a new temptation that he allowed to control his life. When Simon saw that there was a special power present when the apostles laid their hands on people and prayed, he offered money so that he might receive the same power. Simon was failing to realize that true power in prayer comes from living a dedicated life of faith. Instead, he thought it was something that could be bought. Peter rebukes him strongly in Acts 8:20-22: "Peter answered, 'May your money perish with you, because you thought you could buy the gift of God with money. You have no part or share in this ministry, because your heart is not right before God. Repent of this wickedness and pray to the Lord in the hope that he may forgive you for having such a thought in your heart.'" Peter once again is clear that Simon needs to not only ask for forgiveness but also to repent and turn away from his sin.

In Acts 26 Paul is giving his personal testimony to King Agrippa. It is interesting to note that Paul started his involvement with Christianity by persecuting believers. However, through a dramatic experience Paul understands the truth about Jesus and becomes a believer who travels many miles and endures great hardships to see that others hear about the great salvation offered through Christ. Paul is recounting to King Agrippa what he preached to all those people that he traveled to reach with the truth of Jesus. Paul states in Acts 26:19-20:

> **19** "So then, King Agrippa, I was not disobedient to the vision from heaven.
>
> **20** First to those in Damascus, then to those in Jerusalem and in all Judea, and then to the Gentiles, I preached that they should repent and turn to God and demonstrate their repentance by their deeds."

There are three things that we should notice from Paul's statement. The first is that Paul mentions the places that he preached and indicated that the message stayed consistent. Paul says that he preached in Damascus, Jerusalem, Judea and then to the Gentiles. These people groups would have been vastly different in respect to their knowledge, lifestyles and beliefs. Yet Paul's message stayed consistent. He knew that people must believe in Jesus and turn away from sin in order to receive salvation and he taught this to these vastly different people groups. At times we are tempted today to change the message to suit the audience. Some of this is beneficial as long as the core message does not change. We are not helping anyone when we think that a certain group of people will not accept the idea of repenting of their sin and neglect to share this vital truth with them. Paul shared the same message with those who were both used to following the commandments and those who were used to living a sinful life.

The second aspect of Paul's speech to note is that he called upon them to repent. Paul seems to separate the ideas of repenting and turning to God. Turning to God would best be understood as acknowledging the truth about Jesus and trusting Him as the sacrifice for sin. Repenting should be understood as turning away from sin so that Paul preached a message to all those he came in contact with that they should believe the truth about Jesus and turn away from sin.

Thirdly, in the passage Paul states that they should demonstrate their repentance through their deeds. Thus, Paul preached that believing in Christ needs to be coupled with an appropriate change in lifestyle and outward actions. In Paul's preaching, as in the early church in general, there was no place for those who confessed that they had trusted in Christ and yet continued on in a sinful lifestyle. Paul was adamant in saying that faith needs to be proven by a changed life. Thus, Paul makes a clear and conclusive statement to King Agrippa about the way that he preached to people in all of his evangelistic outreaches.

REPENTANCE IN ROMANS

An epistle is a letter written to others and in the Bible God inspired men to write epistles to churches and groups of people to give them direction on how to live the Christian life. Thus, we can also look at the epistles in the New Testament as a way to understand what God desires for us to know about repentance. The first epistle we will consider is Romans. Romans has a lot of deep teaching on the truths of the Christian life and one of the central themes is the avoidance of sin which results from repentance. One of the passages of Scripture important to our study in found in Romans 2:1-4:

> 1 You, therefore, have no excuse, you who pass judgment on someone else, for at whatever point you judge another, you are condemning yourself, because you who pass judgment do the same things.
>
> 2 Now we know that God's judgment against those who do such things is based on truth.

<u>3</u> So when you, a mere human being, pass judgment on them and yet do the same things, do you think you will escape God's judgment?

<u>4</u> Or do you show contempt for the riches of his kindness, forbearance and patience, not realizing that God's kindness is intended to lead you to repentance?

When we read this Scripture it is important to note that God is not telling us that we should never confront someone else about their sin as God does tell us that one Christian should confront another Christian about their sin elsewhere in the Bible (Matthew 18:15-20). Rather, God wants us to understand the danger in judging someone when we are doing the same sins. God then goes on to tell us that His judgment is always based on truth and so God does not make mistakes. Verse 4 reveals to us that one of the reasons for God's kindness to people is to lead them to repentance. As well, this Scripture notes that God's patience should lead us to repent. It seems that God is being clear here in wanting people to understand that He desires for everyone to repent. At times people can begin to think that because God is patient and kind there is no reason to repent. However, God tells us throughout Scripture that those who leave this world without repenting of their sin and trusting in Christ are bound for an eternity without God. God is kind and patient and this should lead us all to repent and not to falsely assume that God will never bring judgment.

A little later in the same chapter the idea of those who are continuing in sin is written against as 2:19-23 reads:

<u>19</u> if you are convinced that you are a guide for the blind, a light for those who are in the dark,

<u>20</u> an instructor of the foolish, a teacher of little children, because you have in the law the embodiment of knowledge and truth—

> **21** you, then, who teach others, do you not teach yourself? You who preach against stealing, do you steal?
>
> **22** You who say that people should not commit adultery, do you commit adultery? You who abhor idols, do you rob temples?
>
> **23** You who boast in the law, do you dishonor God by breaking the law?

Repentance is not specifically mentioned but God definitely is rebuking those who teach people not to do such sinful activities as stealing, committing adultery and robbing temples and yet have not repented of these activities themselves. God again is making it clear that Christians are expected to repent of their sin and have a desire to live a holy life.

Another passage in Romans in which repentance is implied is Romans 6:11-15 which states:

> **11** In the same way, count yourselves dead to sin but alive to God in Christ Jesus.
>
> **12** Therefore do not let sin reign in your mortal body so that you obey its evil desires.
>
> **13** Do not offer any part of yourself to sin as an instrument of wickedness, but rather offer yourselves to God as those who have been brought from death to life; and offer every part of yourself to him as an instrument of righteousness.
>
> **14** For sin shall no longer be your master, because you are not under the law, but under grace.
>
> **15** What then? Shall we sin because we are not under the law but under grace? By no means!

God is desiring for Christians to live a life that is dedicated to Christ and dead to sin. Paul explains what it practically means to live out being dead to sin by stating in verse 12 that we should not allow sin to reign in our lives. This goes against the teaching that some have when they say that once a person has trusted Christ as their savior that it no longer matters how they live. God uses Paul to explicitly address the falsity of this claim in verse 15 by saying that by no means should we allow sin to be a regular and accepted part of our lives. Once again God is making it quite clear that repentance from sin is intended to be a part of the life of a believer both when they first become a Christian and as they continue in their spiritual lives.

Romans 12:1-2 also presents this idea:

<u>1</u> Therefore, I urge you, brothers and sisters, in view of God's mercy, to offer your bodies as a living sacrifice, holy and pleasing to God—this is your true and proper worship.

<u>2</u> Do not conform to the pattern of this world, but be transformed by the renewing of your mind. Then you will be able to test and approve what God's will is—his good, pleasing and perfect will.

Similar to the previous passages in Romans, Paul is directing the reader to present their body as a living sacrifice to the Lord. In the Old Testament an animal that was sacrificed needed to be without any blemish or imperfection. Jesus followed this idea by being the perfect sacrifice for sins or the Lamb of God without any blemish. God is now directing Paul to tell Christians that they need to strive to be holy and to have our lives be like that living sacrifice that pleases God. Verse 12 tells us that Christians are not to follow the sinful pattern of this world and that we are to have our minds continually renewed by focusing on God's truths which are found in His Word, the Bible. This type of a life can be only be lived out by someone continually repenting of their sin and trusting in the power of the Holy Spirit to help them as God progressively shines a light on our sinful attitudes and actions.

REPETANCE IN I AND II CORINTHIANS

The two epistles written to the Corinthians have much of their content devoted to practical teaching and, yet, in these books the idea of repentance is also presented. An interesting passage of Scripture that is often overlooked or dismissed is I Corinthians 5:9-11:

> <u>9</u> I wrote to you in my letter not to associate with sexually immoral people—
>
> <u>10</u> not at all meaning the people of this world who are immoral, or the greedy and swindlers, or idolaters. In that case you would have to leave this world.
>
> <u>11</u> But now I am writing to you that you must not associate with anyone who claims to be a brother or sister but is sexually immoral or greedy, an idolater or slanderer, a drunkard or swindler. Do not even eat with such people.

Apparently in a previous letter God had directed Paul to write to the Corinthians telling them not to associate with people who are sexually immoral. It seems that there was a misunderstanding and now God directs Paul to tell them that avoiding the sexually immoral does not include those who are not Christians. In fact, while He was on earth Jesus exemplified reaching out to those who were not believers as He was known to be the friend and companion of sinners and was heavily criticized by the religious leaders for this. Jesus gave us a model for spending time with those who were not believers and showing love to them in hopes of bringing them to faith.

However, Paul is addressing an entirely different matter here. He is telling the Corinthians Christians that they should not fellowship with a person who claims to be a Christian but is sexually immoral, greedy, practices idolatry (worshipping something other than God), a slanderer, overindulges in some intoxicating substance or cheats people. God is clear that these activities are not acceptable for a Christian and other believers are to avoid having fellowship with people who say they are a Christian but practice these activities. I know that this idea seems harsh but we must trust God's wisdom here. God desires for these people to turn from these sins and if other Christians continue to fellowship with them as if nothing is wrong then they will begin to get used to their sinful life pattern. Of course, the implication, as stated elsewhere in Scripture, is that they may influence other Christians to also engage in these sins.

I also believe that another idea needs to be presented at this time. There is a vast difference between someone who is struggling with one of these sins and someone who has given in to them as if nothing is wrong. For those Christians who are struggling to overcome sin I believe God wants us to strengthen our prayers and relationship with them so that they can be helped in overcoming these activities. However, when someone who claims to be a Christian and practices one of these and is not trying to stop it or resist it then this is the time to break fellowship with them. For example, I know of a couple who are living together and are sexually immoral while at the same time claiming to be Christians and engaging in church activities. It is obvious that they are not trying to fight this sin but have given into it by living together. These are the type of situations that God is addressing here in wanting other Christians to discontinue fellowshipping with them so that they might see the seriousness of their sin.

An important aspect in all of this for our study of repentance is that God is definitely saying that Christians are expected to be actively trying to avoid sin. Actively trying to avoid sin includes the idea of repentance and turning away from any known sin. Another relevant passage of Scripture in I Corinthians that deals with repentance while not mentioning it explicitly is I Corinthians 6:9-11 which reads:

9 Or do you not know that wrongdoers will not inherit the kingdom of God? Do not be deceived: Neither the sexually immoral nor idolaters nor adulterers nor men who have sex with men.

10 nor thieves nor the greedy nor drunkards nor slanderers nor swindlers will inherit the kingdom of God.

11 And that is what some of you were. But you were washed, you were sanctified, you were justified in the name of the Lord Jesus Christ and by the Spirit of our God.

The Lord inspired Paul to tell the Christians at Corinth that those who had trusted in Christ were expected to have a changed life. Again, we must remember that simply living a life without committing these sins is not enough. A person must trust in Christ for salvation and then the Holy Spirit enters and makes the change. However, God wants us to bring to the table a desire to turn away from sin.

The Lord is clearly stating that those who have a lifestyle of sin will not inherit the Kingdom of God or will not reach heaven after passing from this life. The sins listed here are some that are quite common in our culture today, but I do not believe that they are meant to be exhaustive. It seems that any person that has a continuously sinful lifestyle, whether it is one of these sins or another, without being bothered by repentance will spend an eternity separated from God. This goes directly against what many believe today as many would say that as long as someone trusts in Christ then their lifestyle does not matter. God is calling this belief out as being false. The person who has put their faith in Christ will have the result of a changed life and if this has not occurred then there has not been a truly born again experience. In verse 11 Paul clearly states that some of the Corinthians had this lifestyle before they put their faith in Christ. However, now that they are Christians Paul makes it clear that one of the marks of being a Christian is that their life has changed from a sinful pattern.

To some this passage of Scripture may seem harsh but we need to remember that God is doing this out of love. God wanted the Corinthians who may have been a part of that church but never truly believed in Christ and repented to understand their spiritual state. If they did not make a change in their lives then they would not inherit the Kingdom of God. God is making the same call today. He wants us to examine our lives and see what our lifestyle indicates about our relationship with Him. God loved the Corinthians who falsely believed they had a relationship with Him and God loves those today who falsely believe they are saved. He is still calling people to repent of their sins and trust in Christ for salvation.

The book of II Corinthians also has some relevant passages about repentance. One of these is II Corinthians 5:15: "And he died for all, that those who live should no longer live for themselves but for him who died for them and was raised again." God is commanding that those who have trusted in the sacrifice that Jesus made for their sins should attempt to live their lives for Him. This also includes the idea of, as much as possible, being a representation of Christ to the world. In fact, being like Christ is the very meaning of the word Christian. We must then ask the logical question of how Christ would want to be represented to the world by His followers? He would want them to be exhibiting love, good works and avoiding sin just as He was perfect in His time on earth. I know living as Christ would have lived is a heavy task. Of course, no one will be perfect at it on this earth but God asks us to be continually striving, through depending on the power of the Holy Spirit, to have our lives more and more conformed to the image of Christ. Of course, in all this it is necessary that we be practicing repentance.

Another Scripture that presents the idea of repentance is in 7:10: "Godly sorrow brings repentance that leads to salvation and leaves no regret, but worldly sorrow brings death." This harkens back to our earlier study of both Saul and Esau. Each of them seemed sorrowful for the results of their sin without having a godly sorrow. Godly sorrow includes the idea of being sorry that we have sinned against God rather than only being sorry that we suffered consequences. When we have this deep sorrow that we have offended God it leads to salvation but when we are only sorry we suffered consequences it leads to spiritual death.

Another passage that is relevant to our study is II Corinthians 12:21: "I am afraid that when I come again my God will humble me before you, and I will be grieved over many who have sinned earlier and have not repented of the impurity, sexual sin and debauchery in which they have indulged." Paul here is writing to the Corinthian church and reinforcing the idea that people who are Christians are expected to repent of immorality and other sins. However, this is often not the case as many people who say that they are Christians continue in a sinful life pattern and it does not seem to bother them or make them feel uncomfortable. Paul says that he is grieved over these folks that have sinned earlier and not repented and, indeed, every pastor and church leader today should be grieved when activities condemned in the Bible are continuing to be practiced by those who profess Christianity. This Scripture gets to the heart of how we view sin: as a serious matter that needs repentance or as something that is no big deal and can be shrugged off.

REPENTANCE IN THE SHORTER EPISTLES

The idea of repentance is presented throughout the New Testament. We will now look at some examples in the shorter epistles. It is of particular interest that although these epistles are shorter in length that God still led the writers to include the important idea of repenting of sins. One of these passages is Ephesians 4:1: "As a prisoner for the Lord, then, I urge you to live a life worthy of the calling you have received." It is believed that Paul wrote this letter to the Ephesians while he was in prison in Rome and, thus, the reference to being a prisoner of the Lord. Paul is encouraging the Ephesian believers to live a life worthy of their calling. What is the calling they received? The call to trust in Christ as their savior and become a Christian. Thus, as mentioned previously, God is instructing every Christian to live a life that is worthy of being called a Christian. Living a life worthy of being called a Christian would implicitly include the idea of walking in a holy fashion, the way that Christ did, and this must include a repentance and willingness to turn away from sin.

Later in the chapter this idea of living worthily is presented in more detail in verses 22-29:

> 22 You were taught, with regard to your former way of life, to put off your old self, which is being corrupted by its deceitful desires;
>
> 23 to be made new in the attitude of your minds;
>
> 24 and to put on the new self, created to be like God in true righteousness and holiness.
>
> 25 Therefore each of you must put off falsehood and speak truthfully to your neighbor, for we are all members of one body.
>
> 26 "In your anger do not sin" : Do not let the sun go down while you are still angry,
>
> 27 and do not give the devil a foothold.
>
> 28 Anyone who has been stealing must steal no longer, but must work, doing something useful with their own hands, that they may have something to share with those in need.
>
> 29 Do not let any unwholesome talk come out of your mouths, but only what is helpful for building others up according to their needs, that it may benefit those who listen.

Paul opens this passage of Scripture by stating that Christians should 'put off their old self' because they were previously corrupted by sinful desires. In place of the old self each Christian should put on their new self which is to follow God in attempting to live in holiness. It logically follows that in order to live in righteousness and holiness that one must have a continual attitude of repentance of sin. Paul goes on to give several examples of what it would mean to live in holiness which includes avoiding lying, controlling anger, being honest in your work and not practicing unwholesome talk. To achieve each of these areas given as an example would require a continual attitude of turning away from sin.

Later in Ephesians Paul follows this idea of turning from sin with something even stronger. He presents the idea that those who do not turn from sin will not have a place in God's Kingdom as Ephesians 5:5-6 states: "For of this you can be sure: No immoral, impure or greedy person-such a person is an idolater-has any inheritance in the kingdom of Christ and of God. Let no one deceive you with empty words, for because of such things God's wrath comes on those who are disobedient." As mentioned before, this is a strong teaching but it allows us to understand that much of the current idea that anything goes in the Christian life is false and will have consequences. As well, it is not explicitly stated exactly what the 'empty words' are but it can be inferred that it refers to a teaching that a Christian can live a sinful life after they are saved with no negative impacts. In other words, Paul is making a clear point that turning away from sin and avoiding sin are expected in the Christian life.

The epistle to the Colossians presents a similar idea to what was written to the Ephesians as Colossians 3:7-10 says:

[7](#) You used to walk in these ways, in the life you once lived.

[8](#) But now you must also rid yourselves of all such things as these: anger, rage, malice, slander, and filthy language from your lips.

[9](#) Do not lie to each other, since you have taken off your old self with its practices

[10](#) and have put on the new self, which is being renewed in knowledge in the image of its Creator.

'You used to walk in these ways' is a great phrase to encapsulate the idea and essence of repentance. God clearly wants the Colossians to know that once they have trusted in Christ that they are no longer expected to walk in the same old ways. It is interesting that one of the signs of the old life is rage and 'road rage' is something that is talked about so much in our culture. As well, this Scripture mentions 'filthy language from your lips' as being something that a Christian should avoid. It seems that in the last few decades that people are less and less concerned with using 'filthy language' but avoiding it is still a biblical principle that has not and will not change.

Experiencing and continuing in repentance are described as taking off our old self and putting on a new self. One of the things that stands out from this passage of Scripture is that while the Holy Spirit does the changing in a person when they trust in Christ and are born again the individual is expected to bring a willingness to turn away from sin and be transformed.

Paul makes a similar claim about the expectation of a changed life after salvation in his letter to one of the young ministers, Titus, that he is mentoring. Titus 1:16 reads: "They claim to know God, but by their actions they deny him. They are detestable, disobedient and unfit for anything good." Here, God is telling those that claim salvation but do not have a lifestyle befitting of a follower of Christ are actually denying Him by their actions. God has strong words for these people as He refers to them as 'detestable.' This is how God views anyone who refuses to live in repentance and faith in Christ. God also uses John to deliver a similar message in I John 2:1-6:

> **1** My dear children, I write this to you so that you will not sin. But if anybody does sin, we have an advocate with the Father—Jesus Christ, the Righteous One.
>
> **2** He is the atoning sacrifice for our sins, and not only for ours but also for the sins of the whole world.

<u>3</u> We know that we have come to know him if we keep his commands.

<u>4</u> Whoever says, "I know him," but does not do what he commands is a liar, and the truth is not in that person.

<u>5</u> But if anyone obeys his word, love for God is truly made complete in them. This is how we know we are in him:

<u>6</u> Whoever claims to live in him must live as Jesus did.

John begins this passage of Scripture by telling the readers that they should be striving to avoid sin but if they do sin they can have forgiveness through Jesus Christ. He goes on to say that one of the signs that someone is a believer in Christ is that they keep His commands. Again, as we have stated before, the idea of a person being a Christian and yet not being interested in keeping God's commands is foreign to the Bible. I have always felt that verse 4 is one of the strongest and most forthright statements in the New Testament. God states in plain language that the person who claims to be a believer but does not keep the commandments is a liar. Those are strong words but they are the words of God. This serves to reinforce the idea that repenting of sin is important to God.

REPENTANCE IN REVELATION

The book of Revelation spends a considerable amount of time chronicling God's judgment upon the world. The goal of much of this judgment is to lead people to a point of repentance and belief in Christ. Unfortunately, most of the people who experience these judgments still refuse to repent of their sins. We will look at one passage of Scripture as an example. Revelation 16:8-11 tells us:

<u>8</u> The fourth angel poured out his bowl on the sun, and the sun was allowed to scorch people with fire.

9 They were seared by the intense heat and they cursed the name of God, who had control over these plagues, but they refused to repent and glorify him.

10 The fifth angel poured out his bowl on the throne of the beast, and its kingdom was plunged into darkness. People gnawed their tongues in agony

11 and cursed the God of heaven because of their pains and their sores, but they refused to repent of what they had done.

It is sad to think that even when these people understand that God is sending judgment on their sin that they still refuse to repent. A particularly interesting idea is found in verse 9 which couples the idea of repenting with glorifying God. We should understand that whenever we repent of our sin and trust in Christ that this glorifies God. Glorifying God should be the primary goal of our lives and if repenting of our sin will do that then it provides one more reason for repentance.

As well, when we look at this passage of Scripture from Revelation we can see that there are some people who simply refuse to repent. Although they know that the trouble they are having is a direct result of their sin they will not turn away from it. We must be careful that we do not harden our heart when God convicts us. Each time our sin is pointed out by God's Word and the Holy Spirit we need to be willing to turn away from it immediately. Each time we harden our hearts to God's call we are edging closer and closer to becoming like the people described here in Revelation.

I know that much of our study of the New Testament passages seem to be saying the same thing just in different ways. However, it is important to firmly establish the idea that multiple times in the New Testament God speaks about the critical nature of repentance. God wants every reader to understand that faith in Christ and turning away from sin are expected to go together. The idea of a person being a believer in Christ and continuing in a sinful and unrepentant lifestyle is not supported in Scripture.

CHAPTER 5
HISTORICAL VIEWS OF REPENTANCE AND THEIR APPLICATION

Now that we have reviewed several instances of repentance in the Bible we can look at what repentance has meant in different times in history. It is of particular interest to note that people in past times generally had a much more serious view of repentance. Of course, we understand that no one can earn forgiveness as it is a free gift because of the sacrifice that Jesus made on the cross. At the same time, when repentance is taken seriously then it is more in line with how God views the serious nature of sin.

PRACTICE OF REPENTANCE IN THE BIBLE

First of all, it is of interest to understand how people viewed repentance in the Bible. One of the common ways that people expressed their repentance in the Scriptures was with sackcloth and ashes. Sackcloth and ashes are meant to express on the outside what is occurring on the inside. It should be noted that the wearing of sackcloth and ashes on the outside did not accomplish anything unless it was accompanied by a sorrow for sin and desire for holiness on the inside. It is similar to saying today that baptism or confirmation do not accomplish anything unless there is a tandem belief and repentance on the inside. Using sackcloth and ashes, in general, was meant in the Israelite culture to indicate a feeling of humility and debasement. They were also used to show sorrow during a time of grief and loss. Thus, it is especially noteworthy to understand that this symbol of humility, debasement and sorrow was used when someone had committed sin against a holy God.

Whenever sackcloth and ashes were used it was a serious matter. For example, when the prophet Daniel is stricken with the deep sinfulness of the Israelites he repents in sackcloth and ashes on their behalf. Daniel 9:3-6 reads:

> <u>3</u> So I turned to the Lord God and pleaded with him in prayer and petition, in fasting, and in sackcloth and ashes.
>
> <u>4</u> I prayed to the LORD my God and confessed: "Lord, the great and awesome God, who keeps his covenant of love with those who love him and keep his commandments,
>
> <u>5</u> we have sinned and done wrong. We have been wicked and have rebelled; we have turned away from your commands and laws.
>
> <u>6</u> We have not listened to your servants the prophets, who spoke in your name to our kings, our princes and our ancestors, and to all the people of the land.
>
> <u>7</u> "Lord, you are righteous, but this day we are covered with shame—the people of Judah and the inhabitants of Jerusalem and all Israel, both near and far, in all the countries where you have scattered us because of our unfaithfulness to you.
>
> <u>8</u> We and our kings, our princes and our ancestors are covered with shame, LORD, because we have sinned against you.
>
> <u>9</u> The Lord our God is merciful and forgiving, even though we have rebelled against him;

In verse 3 Daniel states that he turned to the Lord and pleaded in prayer accompanied by fasting and being in sackcloth and ashes. This reveals just how serious Daniel considered the sin of the Israelites to be. It would behoove each of us to also have this seriousness about sin. In verse 6 Daniel recounts how God sent the prophets to the leaders but they would not listen. God has sent us His Word and ministers to preach His Word and yet so many times people turn a deaf ear and continue in their sin much like the Israelites. Verse 7 speaks of the severe consequences of their lack of repentance as the people were literally taken into captivity and scattered among other nations. We must remember that God still has severe consequences for those who refuse to repent. In verse 9 Daniel leans upon the mercy and forgiveness of God. It is great blessing to know that God offers mercy and forgiveness for all those who truly repent.

In the book of Jonah we also see a group that of people that repented in sackcloth and ashes. They are not Israelites but nevertheless they follow this custom when repenting before God. Jonah was a prophet and he reluctantly preached to the people of Niveveh. The Bible tells what happened next in Jonah 3:4-10:

4 Jonah began by going a day's journey into the city, proclaiming, "Forty more days and Nineveh will be overthrown."

5 The Ninevites believed God. A fast was proclaimed, and all of them, from the greatest to the least, put on sackcloth.

6 When Jonah's warning reached the king of Nineveh, he rose from his throne, took off his royal robes, covered himself with sackcloth and sat down in the dust.

7 This is the proclamation he issued in Nineveh: "By the decree of the king and his nobles: Do not let people or animals, herds or flocks, taste anything; do not let them eat or drink.

8 But let people and animals be covered with sackcloth. Let everyone call urgently on God. Let them give up their evil ways and their violence.

9 Who knows? God may yet relent and with compassion turn from his fierce anger so that we will not perish."

10 When God saw what they did and how they turned from their evil ways, he relented and did not bring on them the destruction he had threatened.

Although the Ninevites were not Israelites and had limited knowledge about the one true God they still took the need to repent seriously. The repentance was led by their king as it is a blessing to have government officials that lead in repenting of sin. To have a Gentile government leader be willing to lead in repentance by putting on sackcloth and sitting down in the dust is amazing. The result was that God heard their prayer and did not bring judgment upon them. This is a good lesson for us today in that judgment can be dismissed when we are willing to make repentance a priority.

I remember a time in my life when I was also stricken with the idea of my previous sinful attitudes and how much they grieved the Lord. One night I was driving home from a volleyball tournament and I began to think about a way that I had treated a certain group of people for years. It was unfair to them and I did not consider how it impacted them. The drive home was about an hour and the Lord continued to show me the truth about my sin on the way. When I arrived home it was late at night. I did not even wait to go inside the house but I was so grieved at what the Lord had shown me that I opened the car door and laid face down on the garage floor in repentance. I told God of my sorrow in this situation and asked God to help to change my ways in the future. This was not sackcloth and ashes but it was the closest that I have come.

When we look at how people in biblical times viewed repentance, we are reminded of just how serious it is. They understood the gravity of offending a holy God and utilized sackcloth and ashes as an outward vision of what was happening on the inside. Today we do not need to utilize sackcloth and ashes in order to repent but we need to take our sin seriously. God takes our sin so seriously that for us to be forgiven Jesus came and suffered a horrible death as God's wrath was taken out upon sin.

REPENTANCE IN THE 3RD AND 4TH CENTURIES

It is interesting to understand how that Christian ministers and teachers have viewed repentance throughout the centuries. In the early 200's AD repentance was deemed as absolutely necessary. One of the well-known authors from the time, Tertullian, is known to have said: "I was born for nothing but repentance." This is a strong view of repentance but when we think about it there is a lot of truth in this statement. One of our life goals should be to have fellowship with God and we cannot have complete fellowship when there is some sin standing in the way or 'clogging up the pipes.' The way that we eliminate the sin is by trusting in Christ and turning away from the sin in repentance. Thus, we can see how critical repentance is to this. As well, another goal for a Christian is that they become sanctified or live as holy a life as possible. Repentance is also crucial to our sanctification. We can see how an esteemed theologian from the 200s viewed repentance and have some understanding of why Christians from that time believed it to be so important.

When one looks at how Christian writers viewed sin and repentance in the third and fourth centuries one aspect stands out-they took sin and the need for repentance much more seriously that we do. Early Christian writers believed that Christians should be vigilant of sins both committed outwardly and with the mind. As well, they should be careful that their motives are pure. In their writings they called for Christians to avoid sin at all cost, be horrified when sin was present in the Christian and immediately make every effort to repent of sin. Of course, this is in stark contrast to our relaxed attitude towards sin today. While it is true that there is forgiveness of sins through the blood of Christ it does not mean that we should presume upon God's grace as if the sins did not matter or did not hinder our lives. Just like those Christians in the early centuries God calls us to be take sin and repentance seriously. I am reminded of a conversation between two friends that I had knowledge of some years ago. Both of these ladies were in their 60s, were thinking about marriage and claimed to be Christians. In the conversation the one lady made it clear that she and her future husband meant to stay sexually pure before marriage. The other lady, who again claimed to a Christian, said that we no longer have to live by those type of morals. What this lady missed is the truth that the Bible is still the same and sexual purity is important to God. The attitude of the second lady has become so common place today that people do not even think much about it. However, it is still sin and every Christian should be concerned with sexual immorality. The Christian writers of the early centuries would be appalled at such a relaxed attitude towards sin and repentance. The truth is that Christians today should be still be appalled at relaxed attitudes towards sin. Although we may not agree with everything that the Christians practiced in the third and fourth centuries, we should follow them in their desire to stay pure in every way and repent of all known sin.

THREE TYPES OF REPENTANCE

When we think about repentance we can think of it as in three different types. The first is natural repentance and this includes a feeling of sorrow that almost all men have when they have harmed another person. Most people will feel sorrowful when they commit a grievous sin that harms another person. However, this type of natural sorrow does not completely bring the type of repentance that God is looking for. A second type or level of repentance comes when someone has a knowledge about God's divine law and can be thought of as legal repentance. In order to have this a person needs to be aware of God's divine law in some way and this creates in him a fear of God's punishment. A person who has this type of repentance is on their way to the type of repentance God wants but they have not reached it yet. This is based mostly on a fear of incurring God's punishment for their sin. The third type of repentance is what we will call biblical and this is characterized by a person knowing the law of God and not wanting to violate it because it will harm their relationship with God. This is a higher level than simply a natural sorrow because someone has been harmed or a legal repentance because of fear of breaking God's law. With biblical repentance the Christian values their relationship with God and desires for nothing to hinder that relationship.

THE IMPACT OF TRUE REPENTANCE

The bulk of the ideas about repentance shared in the following section were brought into mind by reading what authors of previous centuries thought. Overall, Christian writers of previous centuries had a fuller view of the importance of repentance. It seems that it would be beneficial for Christians today to adopt these attitudes about the seriousness of repentance.

When we think of true repentance we must understand that it is not a passing act. True repentance is not something that we do today and forget about tomorrow. It should be known that true repentance will produce a lasting impact on the future actions that one takes. Of course, this is not to say that someone will never stumble again but rather that when they do stumble they will be reminded and quickly begin moving away from the sinful attitude or action. This leads us to say that repentance is an abiding attitude deep within a person's soul. True repentance produces an aspect of the soul that does not want to sin and this becomes a very crucial part of the individual.

In addition, true repentance produces a determination of soul. In order to resist sin a person must make a determination that they will avoid it. True repentance helps them in having this determination. Finally, true repentance encourages a person at all times to be sorry for sin and to turn away from it. A person who has experienced true repentance will be aware of any sin that comes into their life and quickly make an effort to turn away from it. Thus, true repentance will have a lasting impact that involves an abiding principle to avoid sin, a determination of soul to remain as holy as possible and continual sorrow and turning away from sin. True repentance creates such a desire in a person's life to be holy that even if there was no punishment for sin there would still be a deep sorrow for offending the God that loves them and gave His life for them. Thus, true repentance is something that springs from within a person rather than needing to be produced by others reminding them of their sin. Most of the time the truly repentant person should only need the Holy Spirit and the Word of God to show them their error.

When a person who is truly repentant looks back at their life they will have an extreme dislike for how they used to make excuses for sin. We can all remember a time in our lives when we allowed sinful attitudes and actions into our lives and did not feel driven to abandon them. We used a variety of excuses to placate ourselves into thinking everything was fine and there was no need to change. However, the truly repentant person now understands the error of that way of thinking. They disdain the times when they minimized the impacts their sin was having on their relationship with God. Furthermore, they loathe the times that they made excuses for their sin.

At this point I feel that we should discuss the deep sorrow for sin that true repentance creates within a Christian. True repentance will create a sense of bitter remorse and intense sorrow over past sins. A Christian's past sin is not something to be looked back at as a charming time of fun but rather as inexpressibly horrible. I know these sound like strong words but this is the way that godly people viewed their sin in centuries past and this should not have changed with our times. It seems that it is our acceptance of sin in society today that makes it difficult to have the deep remorse of true repentance. As well, true repentance creates a heavy burden within our souls that can only be lifted when we know that Christ has forgiven us of all sin by His precious blood. True repentance also creates a broken heart within a person as they understand how their sin offended a holy God. I have a close friend who has spoken of his journey with repentance many times. He lived a sinful life for much of his adulthood although he was involved in leadership in a church. In his later years God has called him to true repentance over his past sin and way of life. Many times he has told me how horrifying his past sin now seems to him and of his determination by God's power to not return to it. I believe that we all need to have this attitude about our past sin.

At the same time as being horrified by our past sin we must also bask in the forgiveness that we received when we trusted in Christ and remember that there is no longer any condemnation for those sins. Romans 8:1-3: "Therefore, there is now no condemnation for those who are in Christ Jesus, because through Christ Jesus the law of the Spirit who gives life has set you free from the law of sin and death. For what the law was powerless to do because it was weakened by the flesh, God did by sending his own Son in the likeness of sinful flesh to be a sin offering. And so condemned sin in the flesh." Now that is truly good news. To know that we are no longer condemned for our sin because Christ took the punishment for us.

Therefore, we need to strike a balance. There needs to the godly sorrow and loathing for our past sin that true repentance brings. At the same time we need to not allow our past sins to weigh us down and prevent us from living fully for God now. We need to enjoy God's goodness and forgiveness now while at the same time having that strong inner determination to avoid sin. My friend, if you are reading this and wondering about yourself and your own repentance God is wanting you to consider your life. Has there ever been a time when you realized the horror of your sin and truly repented and turned to Christ for forgiveness? If not, God is waiting for you as He always has been. Trust in the sacrifice that Christ made for your sins on the cross and turn away from sin in true repentance and you will find a relationship with God more wonderful than you ever imagined.

FORCED REPENTANCE

Another aspect of repentance that needs to be discussed is that many people are forced into repentance because of a change in their life circumstances. If a person has only abandoned a certain sin because of changed circumstances then no true repentance has occurred. It is as if the individual knows that the only reason they no longer engage in the sin is because they are not physically or mentally able. They may even look back fondly at the times when they engaged their sinful passion. For example, I think of a person who indulged in alcohol to the point of often being drunk. Perhaps they have to give up alcohol because of health conditions or a lack of access. If they would still overindulge in alcohol if the conditions were different then they have not truly repented. Their repentance is forced because of circumstances.

In the same way there are many people who believe that they have repented because they no longer do the activity. However, this ignores two things. The first is that they would still live out that sin if the situation was different and, secondly, there is always sin that occurs within our minds. Jesus spoke of this in Matthew 5:27-28: "You have heard that it was said, 'You shall not commit adultery.' But I tell you that anyone who looks at a woman lustfully has already committed adultery with her in his heart." This principle applies to all manner of sin in that if we only do not engage in it because we are no longer able to then we are still guilty of desiring it in our minds. When this is the case true repentance has not been experienced. In order for there to be true repentance a person must turn away from sin and not desire to engage in the sin even if they could. Until this attitude is reached the person has not repented and is still under the weight of their sin.

FALSE REPENTANCE

Since we have been discussing what true repentance it is also helpful to discuss some of the aspects of a false repentance. We have mentioned this previously but here we will more fully investigate the idea of false repentance. One telltale sign of a false repentance is that a person has stopped doing their open sins but remains unconcerned about the inner sin that no one else sees. These inner sins may include lust, jealousy, unforgiveness and a host of others. When a person is practicing false repentance they only give up what people can see from the outside while their inner life remains as laden with sin as it ever was. Jesus spoke to the religious people of His day about this very topic in Matthew 23:25-28:

> <u>25</u> "Woe to you, teachers of the law and Pharisees, you hypocrites! You clean the outside of the cup and dish, but inside they are full of greed and self-indulgence.
>
> <u>26</u> Blind Pharisee! First clean the inside of the cup and dish, and then the outside also will be clean.
>
> <u>27</u> "Woe to you, teachers of the law and Pharisees, you hypocrites! You are like whitewashed tombs, which look beautiful on the outside but on the inside are full of the bones of the dead and everything unclean.
>
> <u>28</u> In the same way, on the outside you appear to people as righteous but on the inside you are full of hypocrisy and wickedness.

The religious leaders of Jesus' time liked to look good on the outside but they did not give much consideration to the inside. We must be careful to not simply think about the outward sins that everyone can see but to also be concerned about what is happening on the inside. Those secret sins are just as grievous to the Lord as the outward sins. Dear reader friend, if the Lord has shown you today that you have been practicing outward repentance while ignoring inner repentance then why not turn to Him and fully repent. He is waiting for you!

Another aspect of false repentance has to do with what someone is trusting in for salvation. The individual that has only false repentance will tend to trust in giving up sins as a way to purchase their salvation with their own good works. The Bible is very clear that no can earn salvation by giving up sins. If that were possible then there would have been no reason for Jesus to have come. We can only be saved by a perfect sacrifice, not by making ourselves better or less sinful. Jesus is the only one who could live a perfect life as He was God come in the flesh. Since Jesus lived a perfect life His sacrifice for sins could be for others. Someone with false repentance will often ignore this and trust in their own act of the eliminating of sin from their life to earn their salvation. Their view of the reason to give up sin is completely inaccurate. We give up sin because we are thankful for the sacrifice that Jesus has made and we want to please a holy God not because it earns salvation.

Another common aspect of a false repentance is that there is only repentance as a dread of coming judgment. This is what many people refer to as getting their fire insurance. This type of repentance thinks only of avoiding punishment rather than how much our sin offends a holy God. With false repentance there is no sincere mourning for sin. I think of one type of example that shows how our sin offends God. The Father, Son and Holy Spirit make up the Trinity and they work together in perfect harmony. When Christians, or even people in general, do not work together in harmony it offends a holy God. A person with false repentance will only try to minimize the conflicts they have with another person in an outward way. They think little of the inner attitudes that cause the conflict. A person with true repentance in this area of their life will seek to be in harmony with others because they understand that a lack of harmony is grievous to a holy God. Thus, false repentance only considers the outward consequences without thinking about that needed concern for offending God.

Another noteworthy sign of false repentance is that it is temporary. We all know people who seemingly started off so well in their Christian life only to be soon overcome with temptation and fall back into a sinful life pattern. When repentance is real it tends to be something that is of a more permanent nature. However, a false repentance will not be permanent but rather fade with the passing of time. One reason for this aspect of false repentance is that the individual may be wanting to satisfy their conscience. Once their conscience has been eased with some time of clean living they return to their former sinful state because they did not experience true repentance.

Another reason for this temporary repentance is that people want to avoid some type of trouble. About 40 years ago we knew a family in which the father had been accused of a crime. The family then all went to church together, professed faith in Christ and had a public baptism. After a few months they returned back to their former life. It appears that they were only seeming to repent in order to avoid legal trouble. Once the threat had passed they returned to their former life. They had not experienced a deep-seated sorrow that they had sinned against a holy God but rather only had a false repentance.

A further difference between false and true repentance is who a person blames for their sin and who they give credit to for the good acts they engage in. When a person has only false repentance and they commit a sin they will not accept responsibility but will rather blame someone else for their sin. As well, when they do something good they will tend to take credit for it. In contrast, a person that has experienced true repentance will take responsibility for their sin. In addition, when they exhibit good behavior they will tend to give the credit to God. We can ask ourselves which category we fall into to give an indication of the true nature of our repentance. If you blame others for your sin and take credit for the positive things then it is likely you have experienced a false repentance.

One need to only go to the first man and woman to see an example of this. Adam and Eve experienced a wonderful life in the Garden of Eden while having God's presence with them. However, when they made the decision to rebel against God and commit sin they did not take responsibility for it. In Genesis 3:12 Adam says: "The man said 'The woman you put here with me-she gave me some fruit from the tree, and I ate it.'" Then in verse 13b the woman also refuses to accept blame by saying: "The serpent deceived me, and I ate." Everything could have been different for them if they had accepted responsibility for their sin and truly repented. We do not know if their repentance would have changed their having to leave the Garden of Eden but we know that God desires for us to accept responsibility for our sin.

A further sign of false repentance is who they abhor sin in the most. A person who is truly repentant will find his own sin much more horrifying than the sins of others. However, a person who experiences a false repentance will be much more concerned about the sin in others than the sin in himself. Jesus seems to connote this idea in the sermon on the mount. In Matthew 7:3-5 Jesus states:

<u>3</u> "Why do you look at the speck of sawdust in your brother's eye and pay no attention to the plank in your own eye?

<u>4</u> How can you say to your brother, 'Let me take the speck out of your eye,' when all the time there is a plank in your own eye?

<u>5</u> You hypocrite, first take the plank out of your own eye, and then you will see clearly to remove the speck from your brother's eye.

Jesus is indicating His displeasure with those who are more concerned about the sin in others than the sin in themselves. If you find yourself thinking more about the sins of others than your own sin then perhaps it is a good time to look at your own repentance.

FALSE AND LASTING REPENTANCE: A TALE OF TWO KINGS

When we think of false repentance, the name of King Ahab stands out among biblical personalities. We think of King Ahab's repentance as being false because it was not permanent but lasted just a few years. King Ahab was the king of Israel about 865 BC so he was between King

David and the time the Israelites were sent to captivity in Babylon. King Ahab desired to have a certain vineyard and requested to buy it from the owner Naboth. Naboth did not want to sell the vineyard and so Ahab conspired to have him killed and seized the vineyard for himself. God then sent His prophet Elijah to confront Ahab about his sin. Surprisingly, Ahab seems to repent of his sin as I Kings 21:27-29 tells us:

> 27 When Ahab heard these words, he tore his clothes, put on sackcloth and fasted. He lay in sackcloth and went around meekly.
>
> 28 Then the word of the LORD came to Elijah the Tishbite:
>
> 29 "Have you noticed how Ahab has humbled himself before me? Because he has humbled himself, I will not bring this disaster in his day, but I will bring it on his house in the days of his son."

God is going to give Ahab a chance to avoid punishment because he repented. Two things stand out to me from these verses. First of all, the mercy of God in giving King Ahab a second chance although he was an evil king. God's mercy is great even for those who are the worst of sinners. The second aspect is that the Lord spoke to Elijah about this. How awesome it is to know that we can have a close enough relationship to God that He will speak to us at times and tells what He intends to do. This type of relationship with God is open to everyone if we want it and it starts with a true repentance and living for God with all our hearts.

However, the repentance that Ahab experienced was not permanent as a few years later he has his downfall. We can see that Ahab does not have a good attitude towards men of God when he speaks ill of a prophet in I Kings 22:8: "The king of Israel answered Jehoshaphat: 'There is still one prophet through whom we can inquire of the Lord, but I hate him because he never prophesies anything good about me, but always bad.

He is Micaiah son of Imlah.' 'The king should not say such a thing,' Jehoshaphat replied.'" King Ahab hates the one prophet of God who will tell him the truth and not just what he wants to hear. Unfortunately, hating those who tell the truth is still a common theme today. We can see how Ahab's attitude has changed from the time he repented in sackcloth. This drastic of a change in attitude makes us believe that the repentance was only false and that he wanted to avoid punishment. Often it is a change in attitude that comes before the outward sin and this was going to be true of Ahab.

God's prophet Micaiah speaks the truth to Ahab and warns him not to go into battle. However, Ahab wants to believe his own false prophets and so rejects the instructions of the Lord. He also treats the Lord's prophet Micaiah harshly as I Kings 22:26-27 states: "The king of Israel then ordered, 'Take Micaiah and send him back to Amon the ruler of the city and to Joash the king's son and say, 'This is what the king says: Put this fellow in prison and give him nothing but bread and water until I return safely'" Thus, we can see that Ahab's repentance has evaporated and that he has returned to being an evil man. Of course, Micaiah's words from the Lord come true and Ahab is killed in battle. It could have been different for him if his repentance had been real and stood the test of time. I think the lesson for us here is that false repentance will fade away over time but real repentance stands the test of time.

In contrast to King Ahab we have the events of the life of King Manasseh. King Manasseh lived some two hundred or so years after King Ahab. He was an evil king and probably committed more heinous sins than King Ahab. As well, King Manasseh had a godly father, King Hezekiah, so he did not have negative parenting as an excuse. He was responsible for the deaths of many people as II Kings 21:16 states: "Moreover, Manasseh also shed so much innocent blood that he filled Jerusalem from end to end-besides the sin that he had caused Judah to commit, so that they did evil in the eyes of the Lord." Manasseh not only killed innocent people but he also led the people to commit sins. The leader of a nation should be also be a leader in moral living and Manasseh missed the mark on this. However, his evil did not end there as he even went as far as sacrificing his own children to false gods (II Chronicles 33:6).

God sent prophet after prophet to attempt to warn Manasseh and bring him to repentance but he would not listen. Finally, the Lord sent him into captivity. The king of Assyria even put a hook in his nose and led him to Babylon. While Manasseh was in captivity he came to his senses and repented of his sin. The recording of his repentance and return to God is found in two verses and it is a beautiful portrait of God accepting a repentant sinner. I Chronicles 33:11-12 reads:

> **12** In his distress he sought the favor of the LORD his God and humbled himself greatly before the God of his ancestors.
>
> **13** And when he prayed to him, the LORD was moved by his entreaty and listened to his plea; so he brought him back to Jerusalem and to his kingdom. Then Manasseh knew that the LORD is God.

This is a wonderful a picture of repentance and restoration, however, we saw this before with King Ahab. Remember that the mark of true repentance is that it lasts. How would Manasseh live out the rest of his life after God was so gracious to him? We can look at II Chronicles 33:15-16 for an answer:

> **15** He got rid of the foreign gods and removed the image from the temple of the LORD, as well as all the altars he had built on the temple hill and in Jerusalem; and he threw them out of the city.
>
> **16** Then he restored the altar of the LORD and sacrificed fellowship offerings and thank offerings on it, and told Judah to serve the LORD, the God of Israel.

As far as we can tell Manasseh honored the Lord, and stayed true to his repentance, the rest of his life. We can look at the life of Manasseh and see a beautiful picture of God's forgiveness. Manasseh had committed unthinkable sins as he not only killed many innocent people but also his own children. Many people would say that he should not be forgiven. However, this is not God's perspective. God is willing to forgive everyone of their sin when they repent and turn to Him. If you are reading this and you think that your sins are too great, I will almost guarantee that they were not as horrible as those committed by Manasseh. Yet God still forgave Manasseh and He will forgive you when you repent and trust in Christ.

What a contrast between King Ahab and King Manasseh. Both of them lived sinful lives and were treated graciously by the Lord. However, King Ahab only had a false repentance that did not last. Alternatively, King Manasseh had a true repentance that stood the test of time. We also need to think of this in our times. When repentance does not continue in someone's life then it is false repentance. True heart felt repentance will produce fruit throughout the life of an individual.

REPENTANCE IS NECESSARY FOR ALL

One of the central themes regarding repentance that can be gathered from the Old Testament is that repentance is necessary for everyone. For example, Ecclesiastes 7:20 tells us: "Indeed, there is no one on earth who is righteous, no one who does what is right and never sins." God is clear in telling us that the need for repentance is universal and no one is exempt. The person who believes that they do not need to repent of sin does not understand God in His holiness compared to us. Some years ago I was on a mission trip to Mexico and we were showing a film about Jesus in local neighborhoods and then sharing the gospel with those who came to watch. One of the men I met there has stood out to me for years. He was a local doctor in that neighborhood and a good man by human standards. He devoted his time as a doctor to help those out in this poor neighborhood. We talked for a long time about his need to turn away from sin and put his faith in Christ. Unfortunately, my new doctor friend did not think that he had ever sinned. I would bring up each of the ten commandments and when he admitted to breaking a command he also had a reason for breaking the command and, thus, did not think he had ever sinned. If someone does not think they have ever sinned then they do not have a need for a Savior. I prayed for him for a year and went back to try to find him the next year when we returned. We found his home but not the doctor. He wife was very sad and said that he had died suddenly. He was a young man so this was quite shocking. I never knew if he came to a point of understanding his sin and need for a Savior.

A minister once shared a story about this type of idea in a sermon and it has stayed with me as a good example. A young man had been from a small town and had been a dominant basketball player among the high schools in his area. He had aspirations of playing in the NBA so he went to try out for a college basketball team. When he arrived he found that the other players trying out for the team had all the skills that he had plus they were several inches taller and several pounds heavier. He did not have a chance of making the team when he saw the higher level of competition. It was easy for him to think he was great when he was comparing himself to other players around him. However, he could not compare to those who were at a higher level. What is the spiritual lesson from this? Well, we often compare ourselves with other people we know around us. For some of us it is easy to look like a good moral person when we compare ourselves to others who are also sinful. However, God is not holding a comparison contest where the best 25% of humans go to heaven. No, God says that all have sinned. When we compare ourselves to the standard of His holiness we all fall short. Just like the basketball player who looks great compared to other local players but is no comparison to those who are truly skilled, in a similar way we may feel like we look good compared to others but the real standard is God's holiness and perfection. As well, God requires perfection for a person to enter heaven. None of us have a chance of attaining this perfection and entering heaven on our own. However, God had a solution for mankind. God came in the form of a man named Jesus and lived the perfect life that no human can live. Then he willingly gave His life as a sacrifice on the cross and rose from the dead three days later. Because Jesus had been a perfect sacrifice He could die for the sins of others. Therefore, whoever believes in Jesus as the sacrifice for their sins and repents of their sin receives forgiveness and eternal life. I still do not know what happened to my doctor friend in Mexico. He was truly a good man but he trusted in his own goodness without realizing that his righteousness could never compare to God's. He did not see a need for a Savior because he believed he had not sinned. My hope for him is that sometime in that next year he began to see his sinful state and turned to Christ.

SANCTIFICATION

In dealing with the idea of repentance it is also important to understand the concept of sanctification. Sanctification can best be understood as making a person holy. I know that holy sounds like a lofty concept but we really just need to think of sanctification and holiness as simply progressively eliminating sin from one's life. In light of this, we can understand that there are two types of sanctification. The first type of sanctification is when a person becomes righteous in the eyes of God from the first moment that they trust in Christ. God does not see them anymore but sees the perfect life of His Son Jesus that covers all of their sin. However, God does not desire for our sanctification to end there. The second type of sanctification is when a Christian becomes more like Christ over time. God wants every Christian to strive to become sanctified practically or in how we live our day to day lives. Sanctification is something that will continue throughout the life of a Christian. As we grow in our faith, our knowledge of the Bible and our closeness to God we will continually be shown the sin in our lives that needs to be eliminated. As we progress in our Christian lives the sins should shift from eliminating outward sins to dealing with inner sins of our minds and attitudes. The process should never end but we should always be growing in becoming more like Christ or sanctified. Repentance is important here because as our sin is pointed out by the Holy Spirit and God's Word we should continually be asking forgiveness and actively trying to turn away from sin through Christ's power. It is also important to become more and more knowledgeable about the Word of God and allow that knowledge to penetrate our hearts and change us.

Sanctification should be important to every Christian. It should be our goal to grow more like Christ and please God with every aspect of our lives. If someone claims to be a Christian and sanctification is not important to them then they need to examine themselves to see if they are in the faith. The truly born again person will have an inherent and driving desire to become more like Christ and purge all sin from their lives. There are many verses about being sanctified or becoming holy and one of my favorite ones is found in I Peter 1:14-16: "As obedient children, do not conform to the evil desires you had when you lived in ignorance. But just as he who called you is holy, so be holy in all you do; for it is written 'Be holy, because I am holy.'"

In light of God's call for every Christian to be holy we need to ask ourselves is there is ever a sin in our lives that is acceptable and does not need to be repented of? From the teachings of the Bible we can say, no. Any time that a sin is revealed to us by the Holy Spirit directly or by the Word of God we need to repent immediately. God made us aware of the sin for a purpose and that purpose was so we could seek forgiveness and turn away from it. When we live according to this principle we will be on the journey of sanctification and being pleasing to God.

THE IMPORTANCE OF THE BIBLE

The importance of the Bible would seem to go without saying but perhaps since so many people do not have a good knowledge of the Bible it needs to be said. Understanding the Bible is paramount in our journey of repentance. When we study the Bible the Holy Spirit reveals to us what sin is. As we understand more and more what sin is then we can turn away from it in repentance. However, we need to have that knowledge and that only comes from daily studying the Bible, attending church and listening to Bible teaching from other sources. Repenting of sin should be important to every Christian and the more consistent way that God gives us knowledge of sin is through the Bible. Psalm 119:3334 tells us: "Teach me, Lord, the way of your decrees, that I may follow it to the end. Give me understanding, so that I may keep your law and obey it with all my heart." How does God teach us His decrees and give us understanding of His law? Primarily through His Word, the Bible. As we actively seek to repent of sin and live a life pleasing to God regular Bible study should be a part of that process.

REPENTANCE AND CHURCH

It seems today that being a part of a local Christian group of believers or congregation has become less and less important to many people. However, this is only a modern idea. The Bible still teaches the importance of being a part of a local group of believers. In fact, Hebrews 10:24-25 is clear about it being God's will to continue in church attendance: "And let us consider how we may spur one another on toward love and good deeds, not giving up meeting together, as some are in the habit of doing, but encouraging one another-all the more as you see the Day approaching." God desires for every Christian to be part of a local congregation. Some of the most popular reasons for not attending church that are given is that there are people in the church who are living a sinful life, often referred to as hypocrites, and that people have been hurt by churches. Let's address the first one. It is true that there are hypocrites in every church. There were also hypocrites in the New Testament churches and God never gives any idea in the letters to these churches that it is acceptable for people not to attend. God clearly desires for all believers to be a part of a local congregation and allowing the excuse of hypocrites in the church is going directly against what God has commanded.

A second popular reason for not attending church is that people have been hurt in a church. There are legitimate hurts that occur in almost every congregation and we should strive to not allow that to happen. However, when we are hurt by others in a church it still does not give us the right to disobey God. Also, remember one of the reasons to attend church from Hebrews 10 is that every Christian should be actively engaged in spurring others to good works. We cannot be spurring others to do good works in a church if we are not a part of it.

Being a regular attender at church is also important for repentance and sanctification. God has given every Christian a spiritual gift. God has given some the gift of teaching the word of God and this is useful for us to understand the Bible more thoroughly. The more we understand God's Word the more we will be called to repent and the more we will be sanctified. Thus, it is important for us to attend a church where we can be taught the Word of God to help us have a deeper understanding of sin and be shown when we need to repent. Another positive from church attendance that impacts our repentance and sanctification is relationships with other Christians. God wants us to have close friendships with other believers in a local church. When we have these relationships we can help one another grow spiritually, understand the Word of God and even point out an area of struggle with sin that we might have missed. Proverbs 27:17 carries the idea of helping one another to become better as it reads: "As iron sharpens iron, so one person sharpens another." However, if we do not regularly attend church then we will not have these relationships to help us. An example from my own life was when some years ago I was struggling with jealousy over a situation in my life. It took a Christian friend from my local church to point this out to me and God helped me to repent and overcome it. Again, if I had not been a part of a local church and had that relationship then the help would not have come. As well, we need the prayers of our brothers and sisters in Christ at our local church to help us in our struggles with sin, repentance and sanctification. Therefore, we can see that being a part of a local church is important for repentance and sanctification. The first and most important reason is because God commands it in His Word and pleasing him in every aspect of our lives should be our highest priority. Secondly, God has given people gifts of teaching and this helps us understand what sin is. Thirdly, we need close relationships with other Christians in a local church to both help us identify sin and give us the strength through prayer to avoid it.

TWO QUESTIONS

As we reflect on what has been discussed in this book one of the aspects that comes to mind is how that it applies to us personally. There is a crucial question in how repentance impacts us. When we look at our lives, can we honestly say that we are sorry for every sin? Are we sorry for every sin even to the point that if we could go back to that moment in time we would change everything and not commit the sin? If we cannot say that then we have not experienced true repentance.

A second question we need to consider is in regards to our current life circumstances. Is there any activity, thought process or attitude that the Holy Spirit has convicted us of that we are not actively trying to change and resist? God calls us to actively resist sin. I know that all of us make mistakes and sin but this should not be our normal life pattern. We should be convicted each time we realize there is something in our lives that is not according to what God has commanded in the Scriptures and be proactive in asking God to help us resist that sin. If we are complacent with any type of sin in our lives then we are not living the life God desires for us. As we reflect on the importance of repentance I leave you with these two questions.

APPENDIX

BIBLICAL SALVATION

The most important decision we will ever make in our lives is about our salvation. Therefore, it is critically important to understand what salvation is and how a person can have it. When we think about our relationship with God we need to begin by understanding the truth about what God says about each one of us. Romans 3:23 tells us: "For all have sinned and fall short of the glory of God." To make this point even clearer Romans 3:10-12 reads: "There is no one righteous, not even one; there is no one that understands; there is no one who seeks God. All have turned away, they have together become worthless; there is no one who does good, not even one." God is very clear that everyone has sinned. As well, the penalty for our sin is eternal separation from God as Romans 6:23 tells us: "For the wages of sin is death, but the gift of God is eternal life in Christ Jesus our Lord." This is not just death in the physical sense but also death in the spiritual sense which results in eternal separation from God. At this point it looks very bleak as we have all sinned and our sin brings both physical and spiritual death. As well, there are no amount of good works or attempts to please God that can pay for our sin.

However, God loves each one of us and does not want us to remain separated from Him. God desires that everyone would be restored to a relationship with Him. Our sin stands in the way of this relationship with God. There was only way for the debt of sin to be paid and that is for there to be a perfect sacrifice for sin. Since all humanity has sinned there is no one that could be that perfect sacrifice. Therefore, it was necessary for God to come in the form of a man named Jesus. He was able to live a perfect and sinless life. He willingly gave his life as a perfect sacrifice and was crucified on the cross. He would resurrect from the dead three days later proving that everything he had said was true. Since Jesus had never committed a sin he could die as a perfect sacrifice for others. Thus, anyone who will repent or turn away from their sin and trust that Christ died in their place and took the penalty for their sin can have forgiveness and eternal life. This is biblical salvation and it is offered to all who are reading this. It is not done by any good works that we have accomplished as Ephesians 2:8-9 reads: "For it is by grace you have been saved, through faith-and this is not from yourselves, it is the gift of Godnot by works, so that no one can boast." It is always important that we put our faith in Christ alone for salvation and not depend on any good works that we have done.

The question might be asked about what role good works has in being a Christian. The Bible teaches that we are saved when we repent of our sin and trust in Christ. After we have put our faith in Christ then the Holy Spirit enters every Christian and begins to transform them to become more like Christ or sanctified. Good works come into the picture when we are grateful to God for our salvation and want to please Him by going the good works that He desires for our lives. It is critically important that we do not think of good works as a way to earn salvation. The Bible is clear that salvation is a free gift that cannot be earned. Thus, we must be careful in our thinking and intentions that we are doing good works and obeying the commands because we want to please God out of gratitude rather than using them as a method to falsely earn our salvation.

My sincere hope is that everyone reading this book has repented of their sin and trusted in Christ as their savior. This is the only way God has established that we can have eternal life and live with God forever in heaven. If you have not made this decision yet there is no better time than the present. God tells us in II Corinthians 6:2b: "I tell you, now is the time of God's favor, now is the day of salvation."

www.ingramcontent.com/pod-product-compliance
Lightning Source LLC
Chambersburg PA
CBHW050528170426
43201CB00013B/2125